Michael Colborne

From the Fires of War: Ukraine's Azov Movement and the Global Far Right

Analyzing Political Violence

Edited by Bethan Johnson and John Richardson

1 *Nasser Kurdy, David Tucker*
A Reply to Hate: Forgiving My Attacker
ISBN 978-3-8382-1558-7

2 *Michael Colborne*
From the Fires of War:
Ukraine's Azov Movement and the Global Far Right
ISBN 978-3-8382-1508-2

3 *Dr. William Allchorn*
Moving beyond Islamist Extremism:
Assessing Counter Narrative Responses to the Global Far Right
ISBN 978-3-8382-1490-0

Michael Colborne

FROM THE FIRES OF WAR:

Ukraine's Azov Movement and the Global Far Right

Bibliographic information published by the Deutsche Nationalbibliothek
Die Deutsche Nationalbibliothek lists this publication in the Deutsche Nationalbibliografie; detailed bibliographic data are available in the Internet at http://dnb.d-nb.de.

Bibliografische Information der Deutschen Nationalbibliothek
Die Deutsche Nationalbibliothek verzeichnet diese Publikation in der Deutschen Nationalbibliografie; detaillierte bibliografische Daten sind im Internet über http://dnb.d-nb.de abrufbar.

Cover image: 174883328 © Nicktys | Dreamstime.com

ISBN-13: 978-3-8382-1508-2

Printed in the United States of America

"My mother is the war," declares Roger Mexico, leaning over to open the door.
– Thomas Pynchon, *Gravity's Rainbow*

Table of Contents

Introduction

> We were born in a great hour
> From the fires of war and the flames of gunshots
> We were nurtured by the pain of losing Ukraine
> We were fed by anger and malice to our enemies.
>
> – March of Ukrainian Nationalists

The March of Ukrainian Nationalists was written in 1929 and officially adopted as the anthem of the Organization of Ukrainian Nationalists (OUN) in 1932. From its first lines about "losing Ukraine," the March's sombre yet serious melody quickly pulls you into a defiant ode to war. You're exhorted to defend the homeland "above all else," given that this is a nationalist anthem meant to be sung by fresh young soldiers who have just laced up their boots: "Payment for us is the luxury of fighting! / It is sweeter for us to die in battle, / Than to live in bondage, as mute slaves."

More than eighty years later, this brash call to arms isn't a thing of the past in Ukraine, and not just because an altered version of it was adopted as the Ukrainian army's official march in 2018. A bloody revolution in 2014 and Russia's annexation of the Crimean peninsula, an act not recognized by the vast majority of the international community, presaged the start of war by Russian-backed forces in eastern Ukraine. Despite tête-à-têtes between world leaders and several ceasefire agreements in the years since, the war remains less frozen than still simmering, flaring up every so often to take more lives. It's a war that as of 2021 has taken more than 14,000 lives, including the lives of almost 5,000 soldiers for the Ukrainian side as well as more than 3,000 civilians.

It's also a war that gave birth to one of the most ambitious far-right movements in the world. From its beginnings as a volunteer battalion in early 2014 when Ukraine's armed forces were largely in tatters, the Azov movement was not only born in a great hour, but from the fires of war. A relatively ragtag gang of men from the far right, including open neo-Nazis from Ukraine and abroad, took up arms with blessing of Ukraine's authorities, becoming a battalion, then a Regiment and, eventually, growing into a broader far-right social movement without much parallel anywhere else in the world. Not many of the Azov movement's international allies can boast of, for example, having a political party (National Corps), an erstwhile street paramilitary (National Militia, rebranded as Centuria in 2020), a network of youth camps, multiple social centres, combat sports gyms, book clubs and publishing houses, dozens of affiliated initiatives and projects and, of course, a namesake military unit that's an official part of Ukraine's National Guard.

But the Azov movement's story is, in many ways, a story of all of post-communist Europe. The biggest thumbed nose to the Soviet and Russian legacy in this part of the world has been to (re)embrace nationalism and nationalist organizations of old, like the OUN, to reinterpret national identities to (re)assert power, and where the most admirable trait in a citizen is one's patriotism. The Azov movement, while it's certainly an extreme outgrowth from this soil, didn't sprout up out of nowhere.

My experience covering the far right in central and eastern Europe, in countries like Bulgaria, Serbia, Slovakia and others, led me to the conclusion that Azov is of course similar to other far-right movements. But despite the obvious issues with the far right that exist in these and other countries—including Canada, my home country—Ukraine functions on an entirely different level. The Azov movement is able to operate with a level of impunity their friends in other countries could only imagine: a literal "land of opportunity," as one Azov movement representative once admitted to me. Even as someone who was a latecomer to the proverbial party—I only started to closely follow and cover the movement in the autumn of 2018—it didn't take long for me to realize what I had been missing.

For me, it was the realization that peeling back the curtain of the frontstage—how the movement wanted to present itself—to see the more extreme, hardcore backstage was too easy, perhaps easier than any other far-right group I've encountered before or since. This was all in plain sight, on public social media profiles, in publicly written articles in Ukrainian, Russian and English. And yet, I quickly realized this movement wasn't getting the attention it deserved, in Ukraine or internationally. By 2022, this situation has changed somewhat: there has been renewed international and particularly American media attention on the Azov movement, especially a focus on the movement's alleged role in facilitating international far-right extremism.

Despite this, Azov still doesn't get the attention or scrutiny it deserves. It's not because the information or insights aren't out there, as the many references in this book make clear. It's that these are often scattered around different corners of the internet, not always in English for an international audience, not always widely promoted and not always complete. At least part of this is because, even when journalists like myself from Ukraine or abroad write about the Azov movement, the amount and depth of our coverage and what we focus on varies at times due to resources, priorities and the interests of our editors and our audiences. In part, this book is my attempt to go past that and provide something that will be of benefit both to scholars of the far right and of Ukraine, but also to non-specialists and members of the broader general public who are interested in the issue of far-right extremism.

Ukraine's Azov movement[1] has exploited Ukraine's fractured social and political situation, least of all the still-hot war, to build a powerful and dangerous far-right movement. It has long been able to operate with a brazen level of openness, including with the alleged protection of powerful political figures and alleged involvement in criminal activities. It's a movement that has served and will continue to serve as a model and inspiration for other far-right movements around the world. Its two-faced embrace of violence and its ambitions to be part of an increasingly powerful transnational far right make it a threat beyond Ukraine's borders.

But Azov is not invincible. Their once lofty ambitions of transnational far-right dominance are on hold—for now. The movement's fortunes have clearly ebbed and flowed over time, with

---

1 When speaking of the movement as a whole, I use "Azov" as a shorthand for the entire movement throughout this book, or more often "the movement." When speaking of the specific military unit that gave the broader movement its name, I refer to it as the "Azov Regiment" or "the Regiment."

periods of considerable public presence interspersed with moments of relative quiet. Their alleged patron in Ukraine's powerful interior ministry, Arsen Avakov, is no longer in the job as of July 2021; soon after, some Azov members with alleged involvement in criminal activity found themselves arrested as their leaders complained about a repression of their movement at the hands of Volodymyr Zelenskyy, president since 2019. The movement, however, is still going strong, with no evidence to suggest it's about to disappear anytime soon.

Most of the material for this book is drawn from several years of coverage, research and analysis of the Azov movement. I draw first on interviews with members and senior figures in the Azov movement I've conducted over the past several years, as well as interviews and discussions with numerous observers, experts, other journalists and sources with knowledge of and close to the Azov movement. Secondly, I have made ample use of open source information on the Azov movement, as I've done as part of my work with investigative journalism website Bellingcat, collecting and analyzing almost everything I have ever been able to find on Azov. The amount of publicly available information about and even from the Azov movement, from court records and obscure news articles to semi-private Telegram chat rooms, is simply massive; as is the case with the far right everywhere, it's also woefully underexplored and underutilized. What this book isn't, among other things, is some sort of 'insider' exposé, a dissertation-like account of every detail about the movement or a sort of ethnographic foray into what it means to be a rank-and-file member of a far-right group in Ukraine. These would no doubt be incredibly valuable contributions, but they are not what I've done here.

This book is written from the position that far-right extremism should have no place in our politics and in our societies, and that no amount of far-right extremist rhetoric or actions should ever be considered acceptable. The far right shouldn't be downplayed or outright denied for the perceived good of a country at war. A failure to confront, refuse and reject the far right is a failure to stand up for the values of liberal democracy and a failure to stand up for those in our societies whose lives stand to be harmed most by the far right—among them women, LGBT+ individuals and members of racialized minority groups. No matter if propaganda forces from an aggressive foreign power will make light of it to make your country look bad. No matter if the country is (still) at war. No matter if there are other significant if not more pressing problems governments to also deal with. No matter if far-right extremism is a problem in other countries too.

I don't pretend to occupy some position of faux-objectivity in writing about the far right, whether the Azov movement or any other far-right movement, group or individuals. There is no objectivity or neutrality when it comes to writing about the far right or about anything, for that matter. Claiming otherwise itself serves "an ideological purpose, whether consciously or not" (Mondon, 2020); instead one should acknowledge and always be aware of one's own biases, ready to challenge them at every turn, though I will be first to admit this is not always the easiest thing to do.

I will conclude here by quickly outlining the structure of this book. In Chapter 1 I explore the roots of Azov, discussing Ukraine's past—or at least, how Azov interprets it—the context of the far right in contemporary Ukraine, as well as the revolution of 2014 and how the Azov movement came to be. I move to discuss Azov's ideological inspirations in Chapter 2, exploring the movement' various domestic and international ideological foundations before ending with a discussion of what I dub the core ideological sentiments that underpin the Azov movement.

Chapter 3 is where I discuss what could best be called Azov's politics in practice—how the movement is structured, what its various elements do and, importantly, how we can best understand how the various 'official' and 'unofficial' elements of the movement relate to each other. The murky world of Azov is what I explore in Chapter 4, a world of political connections and alleged criminality that has helped get the movement to where it is today.

In Chapter 5 I discuss how Azov has, with some success, managed to mainstream itself in Ukrainian politics and society despite being extreme to the core; in Chapter 6 I discuss Azov's international ambitions, including how these ambitions have been thwarted in recent years. The concluding chapter, Chapter 7, is where I discuss the future of Azov and Ukraine, and make several arguments for how both Ukraine and the international community can deal with one of the most ambitious far-right movements in the world.

Chapter 1: The Roots of Azov

Stony-faced and in fatigues, the Azov Regiment's then-commander Andriy Biletsky stood in front of his troops in the small city of Chyhyryn in central Ukraine. With his hands behind his back, punctuating his speech with deliberate pauses, Biletsky reached far into Ukraine's past—at least to parts of it a Ukrainian far-right leader like him would do—to draw a direct line to the present.

"Remember," Biletsky told gathered Azov Regiment troops in April 2015, on their way to fight Russian-backed forces in eastern Ukraine, "that you are the descendants of tens, hundreds of generations of heroes going back deep into our history."[2]

"*Upitsi,*" Biletsky said, in reference the World War II-era Ukrainian Insurgent Army (UPA). "*Holodnoiartsi,*" he added, evoking the last holdouts fighting for an independent Ukraine before its incorporation into the Soviet Union, and who did so in the very place Biletsky was speaking.

"Khmelnytskyi's Cossacks, warriors of Sviatoslav and Prince Igor, Scythians," he concluded. "All of them stood guard over our European civilization against barbarous Eurasia."

The Azov movement's immediate roots, of course, lay in the Azov Battalion, a military unit with explicitly far-right roots formed in response to aggression by Russian-backed forces in 2014. But Biletsky's words underscore that the Azov movement's contemporary battles are rooted in a sense not just of their history, but what they feel is their mission based on that history—their duty, or even their destiny.

In this chapter I will first explore Ukraine's past, moving briefly through the centuries through to World War II, the fall of Communism and developments in independent Ukraine in the 1990s and 2000s. Then I will move to an overview of the 2013-14 Maidan revolution—particularly the far-right's much-debated

2 "*Nynishnia viyna na Donbasi - Ise viyna dvokh tsyvilizatsiy: Andriy Bilets'kyy*" ("The current war in Donbas is a war of two civilizations" Andriy Biletsky"); YouTube, April 25, 2015, https://www.youtube.com/watch?v=vkhIE-sAb1c.

role—the subsequent start of war with Russian-backed forces in eastern Ukraine and, of course, how Azov was born.

Kurgans to Cossacks

Some 5,000 years ago, the vast steppes occupying parts of modern-day Ukraine and Russia were the homeland of speakers of Proto-Indo-European (PIE), the language at the roots of the vast majority of Europe's modern languages. Some of these original PIE speakers migrated westward deeper into Europe, dominating then-native populations and leaving the Indo-European languages in their wake. This, at least, is one of the leading hypotheses of where most of Europe's languages came from—the Kurgan hypothesis, named after the burial mounds of ancient peoples in what are now the steppes of Ukraine and Russia.

Recent studies have lent support to this hypothesis. One study (Haak et al, 2015) suggested that between 3,000 and 4,500 years ago there was a massive migration into central Europe from its eastern edges that has left not only a linguistic but a genetic mark on Europe—"almost a total replacement event," in the words of one of the study's co-authors (Curry, 2015). Still, it's only a theory; even the authors of the 2015 study discussed above admit that "the ultimate question of the Proto-Indo-European homeland is unresolved by our data" (Balter, 2015). Some scientists suggest the westward migration from the steppe may hardly have been the domination and conquest that some have portrayed it (Jacobson, 2018).

This might all seem like arcana, of interest only for students or science documentary channels. But all things Indo-European are popular with the far right; for the influential French *Nouvelle Droite* (discussed in Chapter 2), the Indo-European past represents the hierarchical, pre-Christian, 'primordial' roots of Europe which contemporary Europe should strive to emulate. The Azov movement is no exception to this trend, having translated books and hosted lectures and seminars with their own spins on Indo-European studies, including "the importance of Indo-European heritage for the future revival of Europe" (Ostrogniew, 2019).

Another group of ancient Indo-Europeans that lived in much of what is now Ukraine and Russia were the Scythians. A group of semi-nomadic tribes, living between the 7th century BC and the 4th century AD, the Scythians were speakers of an Iranian language, an Indo-European language.

If the Scythians have any reputation, it is as a group of warriors, vanquishing their enemies around them. However, the reality of Scythian life may have been much more sanguine (Schuster, 2021), with a diverse and heterogeneous population, including sedentary farmers, that hardly correspond to the bellicose image of the Scythians we have today. By the 4th century A.D., the Scythians had mostly assimilated into neighbouring populations, and soon, by the 6th century A.D., any remaining Scythians had assimilated into the early eastern Slavs.

By the 8th century A.D., these eastern Slavs had federated into a proto-state comprising parts of modern-day Ukraine, Belarus and Russia: Kyivan Rus', under the rule of Norse Varangians who eventually assimilated into the Slavic tribal population.

The Varangian prince Rurik became known as the founder the dynasty which bears his name. After his death in 879, Rurik's brother-in-law, Oleg, conquered Kyiv and moved his capital there from Novgorod. After Oleg's death in 912, Rurik's son Igor became ruler and earned a reputation as a warrior, with his troops twice attacking the Byzantine capital of Constantinople.

Igor's son Sviatoslav (the Brave) ruled Kyivan Rus' for almost three decades in the 10th century. In 965 the pagan Sviatoslav conquered the Khazars, an empire whose rulers and at least some of its population were Jewish. Sviatoslav, as a result, has become lauded as a "hero" by the region's anti-Semites and the far right (Grinberg, 2021). Sviatoslav may not be a household name in Ukraine, "a barely remembered figure out of school history textbooks" (Petik and Gorbach, 2016). Sviatoslav was nonetheless a man important enough for Azov for them, under Biletsky's watch, to erect a statue in the city of Mariupol in 2015 where one of Vladimir Lenin used to stand.

Thanks largely to the invasion of the Mongols, Kyivan Rus' collapsed in the 13th century, though for all three eastern Slavic states it remains a fundamental part of their national histories. While parts of what is now Russia carried on as fragmented successor states under the thumb of the Mongol Golden Horde until breaking free in the 15th century, their counterparts in most of what is now Ukraine eventually fell under the rule of Poland and Lithuania.

By the 16th century, a new society had begun to emerge in what is now southern Ukraine—the Cossacks, derived from a Turkic word meaning "free man." Along the frontier with both the Tsardom of Russia and the Ottoman vassal Crimean Khanate, this new society became made up of all manner of people, from peasants fleeing serfdom in the Polish-Lithuanian Commonwealth, disgruntled nobles or individualistic adventurers, though the Commonwealth saw the Cossacks as their subjects.

Based in the *sich*, a fortified capital and military centre in the lands beyond the rapids ("*za porohy*" and thus, Zaporizhia) of the Dnieper, the Cossacks developed a reputation as fierce warriors. They defended the frontiers from Crimean Tatar slave raids (and themselves raided Ottoman territories) and also became known for their proto-democratic organization of a general assembly (*rada*) as the highest authority and a Hetman as the highest elected official. The Cossacks managed to earn some degree of begrudging autonomy from the Commonwealth, which largely earned them their loyalty. This loyalty, however, became tested in 17th century in a series of Cossack rebellions, largely because of resentment of Commonwealth authority and religious strife between the Eastern Orthodox Cossacks and the Catholic Commonwealth.

The largest of these rebellions was led by nobleman-turned-Cossack Bohdan Khmelnytskyi. The rebellion began in 1648 when Khmelnytskyi tried to reclaim land that had been taken from him by a rapacious Polish nobleman. But soon, with Khmelnytskyi's political and military skills and in his new position as Hetman, it became a popular rebellion of Cossacks against their Polish overlords. Over the course of the rebellion Khmelnytskyi's Cossack forces committed a number of atrocities against their foes, including the murders of tens of thousands of Jews.

Khmelnytskyi was eventually forced to turn to Russia for help, after being betrayed by former Crimean Tatar allies and receiving no support from the Ottoman Empire in his fight against the Commonwealth. In 1654, in a move which continues to echo in Russia-Ukraine relations to this day, the Treaty of Pereyaslav was signed that saw the Cossacks swear loyalty to the Russian Tsar. The war with the Commonwealth continued after Khmelnytskyi's death in 1657 – in Chyhyryn, the Cossack capital where he was elected Hetman – until the Treaty of Andrusovo in 1667, which split the Cossack Hetmanate in half between Russia and the Commonwealth, with relative autonomy for the Cossacks under Russian authority.

The quest, however, for a fully independent Cossack state continued. In the early 1700s Hetman Ivan Mazepa allied with Russia's enemy, Sweden, for help in a new war against the Commonwealth – and against Russia, in the hopes of independence. It was not to be; at the Battle of Poltava in 1709, Russian forces routed a combined Swedish and Cossack force. Mazepa fled in exile and died. Over the next few decades Cossack autonomy would be slowly restricted under the thumb of the Russian Empire, with Catherine II of Russia abolishing the institution of Hetman in 1764 and in 1775 ordering the Zaporizhian Sich destroyed.

The Cossacks have left an enormous imprint on contemporary Ukraine, often seen as "the embodiment of [Ukrainian] national values" (TRAFO, 2019). Cossack myth and imagery, centred on individualism, patriotism and bravery, has been utilized by forces as disparate as mainstream liberals, Soviet propagandists and Ukrainian nationalists, right up to the present day. For their part, Azov constantly evokes the Cossacks, even framing themselves as the Cossacks' "descendants [who] are also defending Ukraine from the invasion of the East."[3]

---

3 National Corps Kyiv, "*Kozaky vmily Rizdvo sviatkuvaty*" ("The Cossacks knew how to celebrate Christmas"), Telegram, December 25, 2020, https://t.me/national_corp_kyiv/2318.

Ukrainian nationalism's slow birth

The 19th century in Europe, especially towards the east, was full of romantic 'national revivals.' Intellectuals, artists and writers from a number of ethnic groups, from Bulgarians to Czechs to Finns, began searching for a national self-consciousness while living under the thumb of more dominant empires, with little respect from those rulers for their minority languages and cultures.

Ukrainians, of course, were part of this trend. Efforts from prominent writers and artists, particularly Taras Shevchenko, whose role in developing Ukrainian language and culture is omnipresent to this day, helped give voice to a distinct Ukrainian ethnic self-consciousness. The demonym 'Ukrainian' itself only began to be used more widely during this time, with those we now call Ukrainians using the term 'Ruthenian' to refer to themselves (*Rusyny*) and their language (*rusyns'ka*).

The 19th century would prove to be an uphill and uneven journey for Ukrainians looking to assert a national identity. In the Russian Empire, where most Ukrainians lived, the Ukrainian language was banned as a subject and language of instruction from 1804, a ban which was not lifted until 1917. The Ems Ukaz of 1876 even banned Ukrainian in print, save for reprinted historical texts. Ukrainians living in Austrian-controlled Galicia and Bukovyna, however, had more freedom to use, teach and write in Ukrainian.

This unevenness, however, led to the Ukrainian national revival to be less strong and less broad than other national revivals across eastern Europe (Wilson, 1996). As Wilson explains, Ukrainians lacked powerful national elites, and the national revival itself was too confined in regional and social bases to have a significant impact. Moreover, Ukraine's periods of quasi-independence before the First World War were incredibly brief, in the late 1600s under the Cossack Hetmanate, which left little tradition of an independent nation to build upon.

Still, when the chaos of the First World War came to the territories home to millions of ethnic Ukrainians, some of them tried to make an independent Ukraine a reality. The Ukrainian National Republic (UNR) was declared in January 1918, in the wake of the

Russian Revolution. The UNR had a haphazard existence during the chaos of the war, at one time overthrown by a pro-German "Hetmanate" in 1918 that itself held power for just over eight months.

By 1921, however, the war for an independent Ukraine was lost. Ukrainians, once split in two, were now divided in four. Most lands occupied by Ukrainians became part of Soviet Ukraine, while Galicia and part of Volhynia went to newly-independent Poland; parts of Bukovyna went to Romania, while Transcarpathia went to the newly-formed Czechoslovakia.

Some, though, continued to fight. Centred around Chyhyryn, the Kholodny Yar Republic was the last territory held by Ukrainians fighting for an independent state. With control over only a small bit of central Ukrainian territory, it had an army of tens of thousands at their peak, calling its commanders "otomans" as the Cossacks had done. The Republic would, however, meet defeat in 1922, and a number of their leaders executed by the Soviets. Decades later, they would be lionized by Azov's political party, the National Corps, as "another confirmation of Ukrainians' love of freedom, their willingness to fight for it and even pay for it with their blood."[4]

While Ukrainians made up a majority in Polish-controlled Eastern Galicia, they were nonetheless quickly subjected to discriminatory measures and repression from the new Polish authorities. Polish efforts to assimilate Ukrainians in their new territory amounted to "oppression of almost all forms of [Ukrainian] communal and cultural life" (Plokhy, 2015).

Frustrated by the failure to obtain an independent state and radicalized thanks to oppression from Polish authorities, some Ukrainians began looking for extreme solutions to their national question. In 1920, a Ukrainian veteran officer of both the Austro-Hungarian Army and the UNR, Yevhen Konovalets, set up the

4 National Corps, *"Volia abo smert': 98 rokiv tomu vidbuvsia ostanniy biy kholodnoi-ars'kikh otmaniv"*("Freedom or death: 98 years ago was the last battle of the atamans of Kholodny Yar."), February 9, 2021, https://nationalcorps.org/volya-abo-smert-98-rokiv-tomu-vidbuvsya-ostannij-bij-holodnoyarskih-otamaniv/.

Ukrainian Military Organization (UVO). The UVO would devote itself to clandestine resistance against Soviet, Polish, Romanian and Czechoslovak authorities, resistance which included bomb attacks and assassination attempts, some successful.

In 1929 in Vienna, Konovalets used his organizational and leadership skills to unite a number of radical nationalist Ukrainian activists into a single organization—the Organization of Ukrainian Nationalists (OUN). At its foundation, the OUN was an explicitly far-right organization, willing to use violence and terror to meet its goal of an independent Ukraine. Fascists like the Union of Ukrainian Fascists played a central role in the OUN (Rudling, 2011) and its birth followed the trend of similar fascist organizations sprouting up across Europe, like Croatia's Ustashe and Romania's Iron Guard. The OUN was an organization whose legacy remains not only deeply imprinted on contemporary Ukraine, but deeply contested.

The Organization of Ukrainian Nationalists (OUN) and World War II

The so-called "Ten Commandments of a Ukrainian Nationalist," also known as the Decalogue, was adopted by the OUN in 1929. In its original version, the OUN Decalogue instructed members that they "should not hesitate to commit the greatest crime if the good of the cause requires it," though this was softened to "the most dangerous task" in later versions (Rossoliński-Liebe, 2015).

OUN members certainly didn't hesitate to commit such 'great crimes' or 'dangerous tasks' throughout the 1930s. Several leading political figures, including the Polish interior minister, were assassinated by the OUN. They also assassinated dozens of other public figures, including a Soviet official in retaliation for the Holodomor, Stalin's forced famine that took the lives of between three to four million Ukrainians and is recognized as a genocide by a number of countries. The OUN also spent the 1930s becoming close to Nazi Germany, with the OUN even having a representative at an international 'National Socialist' conference in 1937 (Rudling, 2011). As the Second World War approached, the OUN had an estimated 8,000 to 9,000 members (Shkandrij, 2015).

As Nazi Germany and subsequently the Soviet Union invaded Poland in 1939, the OUN openly collaborated with the Nazis, hoping that they would be their ticket to forming an independent Ukraine. In 1940, however, OUN split into two hostile factions—the older and less radical OUN(m) led by Andriy Melnyk, and the younger and more violent OUN(b) led by Stepan Bandera, a group that Timothy Snyder (2003) described as a "nationalist terrorist organization, led by immature and angry men."

Once Nazi Germany invaded the Soviet Union in 1941, the OUN(b) appeared to think that an independent Nazi-backed state, like Jozef Tiso's Slovak State or Ante Pavelic's Independent State of Croatia (NDH), was on the cards. On June 30, 1941, the OUN(b) declared the Act of Renewal Ukrainian Statehood, a declaration which stated this newly-independent Ukrainian state would "cooperate closely with National Socialist Greater Germany…under the Führer Adolf Hitler." To the OUN(b)'s apparent surprise, the Nazis had no interest in the Ukrainians as equal partners, and rounded up OUN(b) leaders, including leader Stepan Bandera, who soon found himself in the Sachsenhausen concentration camp near Berlin.

Even with their leader imprisoned, the OUN carried on. Some OUN members, in conjunction with Nazi forces, took part in pogroms that killed tens of thousands of Jews in 1941 (Rossoliński-Liebe, 2011; Himka, 2010; Himka, 2013; Rudling, 2016). The OUN formed and led the Ukrainian Insurgent Army (UPA) in 1942; in 1943 a campaign of anti-Polish ethnic cleansing in Volhynia killed tens of thousands of Poles (McBride, 2016). Between these and more ethnic cleansing in Galicia in 1944, it is estimated that the OUN-UPA killed upwards of 100,000 people. As the outcome of the war became apparent in 1943 and 1944, the OUN began to scrub itself of openly fascist, anti-Semitic elements of its past, hoping to present itself as a tolerable face for the eventually victorious allies even as members continued to carry out ethnic cleansing. Its trademark red and black flag, evoking spilled blood on black soil, remained.

While the OUN-UPA also fought at times against Nazi Germany—a point often stressed by its modern-day defenders, who also note that some OUN-UPA members were executed by the Nazis— their primary enemy remained the Soviet Union. The Nazis released Bandera in 1944, who promptly resumed collaboration with them (Rudling, 2011). With the defeat of the Nazis and the incorporation of Galicia and Bukovyna into the Soviet Union, the OUN(b)'s fight went underground, continuing guerilla resistance against Soviet forces until the 1950s. Many former OUN members and sympathizers managed to flee Soviet Ukraine at the end of the war, becoming active in the Ukrainian diaspora.

For the next several decades, that which bordered on nationalism in Soviet Ukraine was not tolerated. Any dissent, nationalistic or not, could be demonized as that of a "*banderivets'*"—a follower of Stepan Bandera—no matter the nature of their dissent (Andriushchenko, 2015). After the war, there were varying degrees of Russification and repression of Ukrainian language and culture, repression which was particularly pronounced under Volodymyr Shcherbytskyi's tenure as Communist Party leader in Ukraine in the 1970s and 1980s.

Still, the legacy of the OUN and particularly the image of Stepan Bandera, assassinated by a KGB agent in 1959, remains an incredibly divisive one in Ukraine. It is the consensus of contemporary historians that, in addition to the organization's explicitly far-right roots, at least some members of the OUN-UPA participated in violent atrocities, including the Holocaust. Despite this, a considerable portion of Ukrainian civil society and parts of the Ukrainian diaspora continue to downplay or outright deny the OUN's crimes, and often accuse critics as dupes or agents of the Kremlin. Certainly over-the-top Soviet and subsequent Russian propaganda condemning seemingly almost anyone expressing their Ukrainian identity as a *banderivets'* has contributed to this defensiveness, but a full and proper reckoning of the OUN's legacy, "with no omissions and apologism" (Portnov, 2016) is yet to take place in Ukraine.

Independent Ukraine

Gorbachev's Perestroika breathed new life into Ukrainian cultural life in the 1980s. During the first years of the Soviet leader's restructuring and liberalizing reforms of the stagnating USSR, the defense of Ukrainian language and culture "was among the key issues that galvanized Ukrainian society" (Plokhy, 2015). As the 1980s ticked on, liberalization continued apace across the USSR and gave space for a number of informal opposition groups to emerge in Ukraine. Still, these opposition groups were often branded as 'nationalist' by Soviet authorities, including those that made a conscious effort to distance themselves from and even outright condemn nationalism.

As these opposition groups tried to find their place in a relatively liberalized Soviet Ukraine, the USSR itself didn't have much time left. The Communist Party of the Soviet Union (CPSU) gave up its monopoly on political power in 1990s and lost elections in six Soviet republics, and pushes for independence from these and other republics grew even stronger.

In the midst of this, in August 1991 Communist anti-reformist hardliners in Moscow attempted a coup to restore centralized Soviet power. The coup failed miserably. Soon after, Ukraine's parliament, the Verkhovna Rada, passed a declaration of independence on August 24, 1991, a date celebrated today as Ukraine's Independence Day. In a referendum later that year on December 1, 92 per cent of Ukraine's supported the declaration; by the end of 1991, the Soviet Union no longer existed and Ukraine was, finally, an independent state.

The challenge, however, was just beginning for Ukraine. As Wilson (1996) observes, an independent Ukraine had only existed in the late 1600s (the Cossack Hetmanate) and from 1917 to 1920 (UNR), neither of which had "firm control [or...] control over territories of modern-day Ukraine." The challenge for Ukraine's new leaders was to form not only a modern state, but a modern nation.

How was this nation going to be formed? So-called "national democrats" were relatively moderate political forces who championed democracy and tried to combine liberal and nationalist rhetoric. While these forces remained the most significant and would hold the levers of power in Ukraine, nationalists who "questioned or simply rejected liberal solutions" (Olszański, 2011) and held no compunction about using radical nationalist rhetoric soon split from this 'national democratic' tendency and created new and more radical far-right organizations (Andriushchenko, 2015).

Even from a position in a minority, these far-right organizations were able to push at least part of their agendas into the public space; Wilson (1993) notes that topics that were first raised by the far-right (e.g., the retention of nuclear weapons by Ukraine), would soon be picked up by the more mainstream right-wing and then, a few months later, become part of government discourse. Topics that had for years remained the domain of the far right (e.g., positive recognition of the role of the OUN/UPA) soon became part of mainstream discourse (Andriushchenko, 2015).

In this climate several far-right nationalist groups emerged. One of them was the Social-National Party of Ukraine (SNPU), established in 1991. Their logo combined what they said were the Ukrainian Cyrillic letters I and N—standing for *Ideia Natsii,* "Idea of the Nation"—but bore more than a passing resemblance to a Wolfsangel, a symbol used by a number of Nazi German military units and post-war neo-Nazi groups around the globe, including the U.S.'s Aryan Nations. SNPU was "openly racist" in its rhetoric (Olszański, 2011); episodes like an appearance by SNPU members in September 1993 at a protest in front of Ukraine's parliament clad in black uniforms did little to dispel accusations that the party was an unabashed neo-Nazi group.

The party achieved little success at the ballot box; electing only handful of local elected officials in western Ukraine. Outside of electoral politics, however, SNPU stayed hard at work, forming connections with other far-right parties across Europe, including a meeting with Jean-Marie Le Pen of France's National Front in 2000. SNPU also recruited far-right football hooligans into their ranks, trying to build themselves up into a street force. In 1999, SNPU formally established a paramilitary youth wing, Patriot of Ukraine, led by Andriy Parubiy.

Still, the SNPU continued to decline, and by the early 2000s had fewer than 1,000 members and less hope than ever at the ballot box. Party leader Oleh Tyahnybok reformed the party and moderated its image, shedding the Wolfsangel logo and disposing of Patriot of Ukraine. This new party would become known as Svoboda.

Patriot of Ukraine, though, would live on. In 2006 it was officially legally re-registered and re-formed in Kharkiv under the leadership of Andriy Biletsky, a former SNPU member who would have nothing to do with the party's moderating reforms. By then Biletsky, aged 27, was already a veteran of Ukraine's far-right scene since the late 1990s, including involvement in the explicitly anti-Semitic Interregional Academy of Personnel Management (MAUP in Ukrainian) an institution which awarded infamous American white supremacist David Duke a doctorate. Under Biletsky's leadership Patriot of Ukraine and its political party, Social-National Assembly (SNA) became notorious for its open racism, anti-Semitism and unabashed neo-Nazi rhetoric—replete with references to things like "[disposing] of non-White impurity" and Biletsky's own claim in 2007 that Ukraine's mission was to "lead the White races of the world in a final crusade…against Semite-led Untermenschen"[5].

During Patriot of Ukraine's heyday in the late 2000s, the governor of its hometown Kharkiv region was Arsen Avakov. Born to an Armenian family in Soviet Azerbaijan and moving to Ukraine as a toddler, Avakov became a businessman in Kharkiv in the 1990s, making his money in the frenzied post-Soviet privatization of state assets—and even being accused of involvement in the death of a business partner, which he has denied. Entering politics in the early 2000s, it was under Avakov's watch that Patriot of Ukraine prospered. Biletsky and his comrades violently attacked minorities and took part in raids on companies and businesses associated with opponents of Avakov and allies. Researcher of the far right Vyacheslav Likhachev described Patriot of Ukraine as an organization that "systematically cultivated violence as a legitimate method of political activity for years" (quoted in Bereza, 2014).

In one series of raids in 2010, Patriot of Ukraine members took over dozens of newspaper kiosks belonging to a rival of an Avakov ally—an alleged Patriot of Ukraine bankroller—who soon took

5 Biletsky has denied making this statement, blaming it on Russian propaganda (cf. Umland, 2019), but his denials are entirely unconvincing. The statement in question is available on Patriot of Ukraine pages under his name which were archived in 2008, and other websites that predate 2013-14. Cf. https://bit.ly/3DcAmzM; https://bit.ly/3koxJT5.

ownership of the kiosks (Shekhovtsov, 2014). Even after Avakov was removed as regional governor in 2010, his relationship with Patriot of Ukraine persisted; he was supported in his subsequent yet unsuccessful bid to become Kharkiv mayor by a football hooligan with ties to Patriot of Ukraine (Shekhovtsov, 2014).

Biletsky and Patriot of Ukraine soon fell on hard times. In August 2011 several Patriot of Ukraine members were charged in the so-called "Vasylkiv terrorists" case. They were charged, imprisoned awaiting trial and eventually convicted in 2014 of trying to blow up a statue of Vladimir Lenin in a spectacle Patriot of Ukraine's supporters claimed was a show trial, especially since the statue had been removed by local authorities months before the men were even charged.

Soon after, two leaders of the organization, Ihor Mykhailenko and Vitaliy Kniazheskyi, were arrested on attempted murder charges after a fight in August 2011 at Patriot of Ukraine's offices that left a local man with stab wounds and severe head injuries. Mikhailenko and Kniazheskyi were themselves wounded by the armed man, Serhii Kolesnyk, who according to Patriot of Ukraine had attacked their office. Kniazheskyi would testify in court that Biletsky had encouraged Patriot of Ukraine members to kill Kolesnyk, which led to Biletsky attacking Kniazheskyi.

In December 2011, a month after surviving an apparent attempt on his own life, Biletsky was arrested for murder and put in prison to await trial. None of the organization's leadership would be able to personally take part in what was to come next.

Maidan

What would become known as Euromaidan, or the Revolution of Dignity, began on November 21, 2013. Earlier that day President Viktor Yanukovych decided not to sign a planned Association Agreement with the European Union, an agreement that its supporters hoped would move Ukraine further away from the influence of Russia. As a result, protests soon began on *Maidan Nezalezhnosti* (Independence Square) in central Kyiv, commonly referred to simply as 'Maidan' or 'the Maidan' in English.

By 2013 Yanukovych had become the overseer of an almost comically corrupt regime in Ukraine. His family and associates stole billions of dollars from Ukraine's state coffers, and he earned international condemnation for locking up opposition leader and former Prime Minister Yulia Tymoshenko on corruption charges most saw as politically motivated. A 'European future' for Ukraine, the early protesters believed, was one free from the corruption, nepotism and lack of opportunity that plagued life in Ukraine.

The first protests in November 2013 were relatively small, with protesters' grievances ranging from a desire for greater integration with the European Union to demands for broader social and political change in Ukraine (Onuch, 2015). A rally in Kyiv hosted by opposition parties on November 24, 2013 brought the largest crowd to that date during the nascent protests, estimated at up to 100,000 participants.

As the end of November 2013 neared, the protests looked to be dwindling. But the Yanukovych regime's ham-handed yet brutal repression gave the protests an ironic burst of new energy. On November 30, the Berkut riot police violently cleared the Maidan of protesters, which led to even larger protests against Yanukovych on December 1, drawing an estimated 400,000 and 800,000 participants in Kyiv (Onuch and Sasse, 2016).

It was also on December 1 when the far right began to make its mark on the burgeoning protests. At Ukraine's presidential administration building an estimated 200 members of far-right groups – including Patriot of Ukraine members wearing yellow armbands emblazoned with its Wolfsangel logo – attacked riot police. With a commandeered bulldozer charging at the line of police and even a football hooligan who would later become a soldier in the Azov Regiment swinging a long metal chain, some speculated the attacks might even have been a pro-Russian provocation intended to discredit the protests (Risch, 2021). Nonetheless, the day would be played up by the Azov movement in the following years as *den' provokatora* – Provocateur's Day

The protests ebbed and flowed in intensity over the next few weeks until, once again, the Yanukovych regime provoked chaos. Ukraine's parliament, controlled by Yanukovych's party and allies, forced through a series of draconian laws on January 16, 2014 that largely criminalized protest against his regime. In response, some protesters tried to make their way up nearby Hrushevskyi Street towards Ukraine's parliament building, confronting Berkut riot police as well as thugs hired by the Yanukovych regime. At the forefront of these confrontations were young men from the far right. Clad in paramilitary dress with red and black armbands and identified as Right Sector – the umbrella far-right group at Maidan that included Patriot of Ukraine and other fringe outfits – they hurled stones and Molotov cocktails and set police buses on fire. Over the next several days at least three people died because of the actions of police, with many more injured (Onuch and Sasse, 2016).

After these events, the relatively small minority of far-right activists on Maidan began to gain strength and influence in the protests. However, it's clear they were always a minority. Right Sector, by its own estimates, had between 300 to 500 activists (Likhachev, 2015); Onuch and Sasse (2016) suggested that members of far-right groups made up at most between 10 to 20 per cent of protesters during periods of violence in the protests.

However, this minority of far-right activists on Maidan soon began to wield more influence that their numbers might have warranted. With experience in street violence and clashes with police – many coming from a background in football hooliganism – they ironically became invaluable in confronting the violence of the regime. Several mainstream liberal activists told Onuch and Sasse (2016) that, from this point in the protests, they "felt they had to compete and even collaborate with the [far-right] extremist groups…when vying for the attention of possible recruits" for the protests.

In the words of one liberal activist, discussing Patriot of Ukraine:

> "They are radicals but without them we would not have coped, it's for sure. Because we were too liberal. They understood what it could lead to, they predicted aggression from the police. They understood all this stuff and they were prepared for it. We were not. They knew how to organize the tent camp, how to make fire in the barrels…how to defend it, how to put on the guards and so on." (quoted in Ishchenko, 2020)

As the protests drifted into February 2014, those on Maidan became imbued with a more "militant and uncompromising" mentality vis-à-vis the violent Yanukovych regime, thanks to regime efforts to provoke and sustain violence (Risch, 2021). On the night of February 18, 2014, Berkut riot police violently stormed the Maidan. The Trade Unions Building, used as a headquarters for Maidan activists, burned down. The bloodiest day of the revolution came on February 20, when approximately 50 people were shot and killed, with most victims being protesters (some of whom were themselves armed) coming under fire from snipers as they tried to advance up the street from the Maidan towards Ukraine's parliament building.

Subsequent EU-brokered attempts to broker an agreement that included a transitional government and early elections was rejected by those on the Maidan. On February 22, abandoned by security forces and disavowed by his party and allies, Yanukovych finally fled Kyiv, soon making his way to Russia. In all, more than a hundred people died during events in Kyiv, including 13 police officers. and more than 2,500 people were injured.

The role of the far right on Maidan in 2014 was hotly disputed at the time and continues to be so today. While at all times a minority, the far-right's presence on Maidan was often played up and discussed at length by Russian state media outlets and commentators, going so far as to falsely call the events of February 2014 a 'fascist coup.' In 2021, Russian president Vladimir Putin was still referring to the events on Maidan as a "bloody coup."

It's important to note that this hyping up of the far right's role itself has deeper roots in Ukraine. In the 2000s, opponents of Viktor Yushchenko "deliberately exaggerated" the far right's support of him (Andriushchenko, 2015); in 2004, a fringe far-right group held a protest in apparent vocal support of Yushchenko replete with Nazi salutes. But it was a protest in name only, led by a "provocateur" with alleged links to pro-Russian oligarch Viktor Medvedchuk, intended to discredit Yushchenko (Coynash, 2020). A history of manipulative episodes like these has left many Ukrainians and their international supporters wary of any claims made about the far right on Maidan and in Ukraine generally.

Conversely, the role of the far right on Maidan has been minimized or downplayed by its supporters in Ukraine and beyond; one public letter in 2014 urged international journalists and commentators, "especially those on the political left," to "be careful" when writing about the far right to avoid the issue becoming exploited by Russian propaganda.[6] Nonetheless, it has become increasingly clear looking back at the events of early 2014 that the far right, while at all times a minority whose views were not necessarily shared by other protesters, was critical to keeping the Maidan from being crushed by Yanukovych's police. It is also clear that, after Yanukovych's fall from power, the far right had already begun to view itself as the revolution's vanguard—a view of themselves that would be solidified in the fires of war.

War in Donbas and Azov's birth

In the wake of the revolution, Ukraine's government and even its state had to be almost entirely rebuilt from the ground up. A new cabinet was formed which initially included four representatives of Svoboda and others with a past on the far right, including SNPU founder Andriy Parubiy, by now a member of the mainstream Fatherland (*Batkivshchyna*) party of the recently-released Yulia Tymoshenko.

With an aggressive Vladimir Putin on their doorstep, keen to keep a seemingly western-leaning Ukraine within what he felt was Russia's rightful sphere of influence, the new cabinet would soon become a war cabinet. Within weeks, Crimea had been annexed by Russia in a referendum widely denounced as a sham by the international community. In early April 2014, Russian-backed uprisings in Donbas, a heavily industrial, largely Russian-speaking part of Ukraine that was former president Yanukovych's base, began a war that risked bringing Ukraine to its knees.

---

6 "Kyiv's Euromaidan is a liberationist and not extremist mass action of civic disobedience," https://www.change.org/p/to-journalists-commentators-and-analysts-writing-on-the-ukrainian-protest-movement-euromaidan-kyiv-s-euromaidan-is-a-liberationist-and-not-extremist-mass-action-of-civic-disobedience.

Andriy Biletsky and other leaders of Patriot of Ukraine were released from jail in February 2014 under a post-Maidan amnesty for 'political prisoners.' It didn't take them long to get involved in Ukraine's burgeoning new conflict: a shootout between pro-Russian forces allegedly trying to attack Patriot of Ukraine's Kharkiv headquarters left two of the pro-Russians dead.

But Biletsky and his comrades wanted to do more. Ukraine's military was in tatters, underfunded and unprepared for any significant conflict on its soil. It certainly didn't hurt matters that Ukraine's new post-Maidan interior minister was Arsen Avakov, Biletsky's ally in Kharkiv in the 2000s.

According to interior minister advisor Anton Gerashchenko (2016), in April 2014 Biletsky wanted Patriot of Ukraine to be allowed to take up arms in eastern Ukraine against pro-Russian insurgents, but weren't willing to officially take an oath and join the police or Ukraine's National Guard, both of which fell under Avakov's jurisdiction. Within a few weeks, as Russian-backed pseudo-states in eastern Ukraine were about to hold sham independence referendums, Biletsky came around. In Gerashchenko's sympathetic telling, "about 100 young patriots took an oath and got weapons in their hands." The Azov Battalion, officially a special purpose battalion within the interior ministry, was born.

It was along the coast of the Sea of Azov—the source of the battalion's name—that Biletsky and his comrades would make a name for themselves. At the time, the industrial port city of Mariupol, home to some 500,000 people, was under the control of a band of pro-Russian separatists. Interior minister advisor Gerashchenko (2015) stated that, in a meeting between himself, Avakov and acting governor of Donetsk Oblast Serhiy Taruta, it was agreed that available army and National Guard forces wouldn't be able to push the pro-Russian forces out of the city. The only answer, they said, was the nascent Azov Battalion.

A group of volunteers moved from the Cossack (*Kozatskiy*) Hotel in central Kyiv, a former hotel used as an activist base during Maidan and afterwards as an Azov mobilization point and headquarters, to train in Berdiansk on the coast of the Sea of Azov. In all some 150 to 200 fighters trained for several weeks under the watchful of eye of experienced fighters—including Sergei Korotkikh, a Russian-Belarusian neo-Nazi who had reportedly fought in several foreign conflicts. The fighters included a significant number of individuals from Ukraine's far-right football hooligan scene, estimated from 50 per cent (Fedorenko and Umland, 2020) to 65 per cent (Montague, 2019) of Azov's fighters at the time. Other fighters included open neo-Nazis from foreign countries, especially Russia, and reports of the neo-Nazi origins of the Battalion and a significant number of its fighters garnered significant western media attention (I discuss this further in Chapter 6).

In June 2014, the Azov Battalion scored what it continues to promote as its first major victory. With approximately 150 fighters in tow, along with two other National Guard companies and other special forces, Azov helped flush between 60 to 80 pro-Russian militants out of Mariupol, which restored Ukrainian government control of the city. Azov's efforts to liberate Mariupol in 2014 are, to this day, frequently mentioned and written about by the movement, with senior representatives going so far as to say that Azov's efforts "reversed the course" of the war.[7]

Azov's fighters took part in a number of other battles over 2014 and 2015. A number of Azov fighters died at Ilovaisk, part of a cauldron of encircled Ukrainian forces slaughtered by pro-Russian forces in August 2014. Human rights watchers have made several accusations of war crimes committed by Azov soldiers in 2014 and early 2015, which included torture and looting of civilian homes (OHCHR, 2016).

The then-Battalion would grow fast. From some 50 participants at the time of the first clashes with pro-Russians in March 2014 (Gomza and Zajaczkowski, 2019), by the end of summer 2014 the Azov Battalion comprised some 400 to 450 soldiers (Umland, 2019). By November 2014, when it was officially incorporated into

---

7 cf. Landmark Publishing (*Vydavnytstvo Oriientyr*), "*Vyzvolennia Mariupolia stalo pershym real'nym krokom do Ukrayins'koyi Peremohy…*" ("The liberation of Mariupol was the first real step towards Ukrainian victory…"), Telegram, May 15, 2021, https://archive.ph/cAltz.

Ukraine's National Guard as a Special Purpose Regiment, it had a strength of some 800 soldiers (Umland, 2019).

In early 2015, the Azov Regiment would lead an offensive at Shyrokyne, east of Mariupol, in an attempt to push back pro-Russian forces who were launching rocket attacks on the city. While a second ceasefire agreement, Minsk II, was signed in February 2015 (Minsk I, signed in September 2014, had collapsed) fighting slowed down but did not cease, including around Mariupol. Azov and other volunteer units were pulled from the front lines in August 2015, by which time almost 40 Azov fighters had lost their lives at the front. Azov would not go back to the front until February 2019.

But Biletsky and his comrades were interested in much more than just military matters. In 2014, before his election to Ukraine's parliament in a single-member district in Kyiv, Biletsky announced plans to create "a massive youth movement" based around the military unit he led (quoted in Lelych, 2014).

"This movement will outgrow the Azov Battalion," Biletsky said. It would be, he said, "all-encompassing": sports clubs, so-called patriotic education and everything in between. Soon after, in 2015, the Azov Civil Corps was formed, a broader social movement that did everything from host marches and protests to disrupt anti-fascist rallies. This movement would quickly expand: in October 2016, the Civil Corps gave way to the National Corps, a political party that, at least on its face, eschewed the more radical imagery and rhetoric of its forebears. The National Militia (*Natsionalni Druzhyny*) was formed in 2017 as a quasi-paramilitary street patrol and, in the words of one senior Azov representative (quoted in Colborne, 2019c), an "affiliated paramilitary structure" (it would be rebranded as Centuria in 2020). Alongside this, other projects that had begun over the previous few years, from youth camps and sports training to publishers and book clubs, continued to not only expand, but dominate Ukraine's far-right scene and make the Azov movement the envy of far-right activists around the world.

"Yevhen Konovalets succeeded in making a single nationalist structure in 1929," Biletsky said in November 2018 about the Azov movement (Vuiets et al, 2018). "I believe we can do it now."

Ukraine's National Guard as a Special Purpose Regiment. It had a strength of some 800 soldiers (Umland, 2019).

In early 2015, the Azov Regiment would lead an offensive at Shyrokyne, east of Mariupol, in an attempt to push back pro-Russian forces who were launching rocket attacks on the city. While a second ceasefire agreement, Minsk II, was signed in February 2015 (Minsk I, signed in September 2014, had collapsed) fighting slowed down but did not cease, including around Mariupol. Azov and other volunteer units were pulled from the front lines in August 2015, by which time almost 40 Azov fighters had lost their lives at the front. Azov would not go back to the front until February 2019.

But Biletsky and his comrades were interested in much more than just military matters. In 2014, before his election to Ukraine's parliament in a single-member district in Kyiv, Biletsky announced plans to create a "massive youth movement" based around the military unit he led (quoted in Likhachev, 2014).

"The movement will outgrow the Azov Battalion," Biletsky said. It would be, he said, "all-encompassing": sports clubs, so-called patriotic education and everything in between. Soon after, in 2015, the Azov Civil Corps was formed, a broader social movement that did everything from host marches and protests to disrupt anti-fascist rallies. This movement would quickly expand: in October 2016, the Civil Corps gave way to the National Corps, a political party that, at least on its face, eschewed the more radical imagery and rhetoric of its forebears. The National Militia (Natsionalni Druzhyny) was founded in 2017 as a quasi-paramilitary street patrol and, in the words of one senior Azov representative (quoted in Colborne, 2019), an "affiliated paramilitary structure" (it would be rebranded as Centuria in 2020). Alongside this, other projects that had begun over the previous few years (from youth camps and sports training to publishers and book clubs) continued to not only expand but dominate Ukraine's far-right scene and make the Azov movement the envy of far-right activists around the world.

"Yevhen Konovalets succeeded in uniting a single nationalist structure in 1929," Biletsky said in November 2018 about the Azov movement (Vynets et al., 2018). "Today, we can continue."

Chapter 2: Ideologies and Inspirations

As if trying to look as scholarly as possible, Mykola Kravchenko stood at the podium in a sport coat and turtleneck sweater to deliver a presentation titled 'The Concept of Multilevel Citizenship.'

Kravchenko, described in numerous official Azov movement social media posts as the "chief ideologue" of the Azov movement, was speaking at the Bandera Readings (*Banderivs'ki chytannia*) in January 2021, an event that describes itself as "the largest intellectual nationalist event in Ukraine."[8] A vertical banner with Bandera's face, a stony gaze at the podium, flanked one side of the room as a life-sized cardboard cutout of the OUN leader stood watch from the other.

A dozen or so attendees sat there in a meeting room at the information and exhibition centre of the Maidan Museum, in the rebuilt Trade Unions Centre building gutted by fire in 2014. What Kravchenko said to them there, and to those watching online, sounded as clunky and awkward as the title projected up behind him.

"The regime of liberal totalitarianism that presently dominates the system of international relations absolutizes the concept of universal suffrage," Kravchenko began. "This is the main reason for the very real deconstruction of the institution of national statehood."[9]

The Azov ideologue and former senior member of Patriot of Ukraine would go on to argue that the right to vote should not only be limited to a select group of people, but that some votes – including votes from military veterans like himself – should be given more weight than others. Kravchenko went on to lament the lack of an "effective system" to take away civil rights, which he argued

8 *Banderivs'ki chytannya* ("Bandera readings"), Facebook, https://www.facebook.com/bandera.chyt/.

9 *VIII Banderivs'ki chytannya: Ukrayins'kyy natsionalizm v suchasnomu protystoyanni / Usi vystupy i dopovidi* ("VIII Bandera readings: Ukrainian nationalism in modern confrontation / All speeches and reports"), YouTube, January 30, 2021, https://www.youtube.com/watch?v=pmHdGi6zcWY&t=22561s.

should be given based solely on merit, or even to take away one's citizenship.

None of this explicitly anti-democratic language was anything new. Kravchenko's lecture, as he himself stressed, was based on the concept of "natiocracy" (*natsiokratiia*), an Italian Fascist-inspired theory of a hierarchical, elitist and dictatorial political system laid out by OUN ideologue Mykola Stsiborskyi in 1935.

But the Azov movement draws ideological inspiration from much more than just 1930s-era pro-Fascists. As I discuss in this chapter, it is an ideologically heterogenous far-right movement, drawing influences and inspirations in varying degrees—and on varying parts of the movement—from Ukrainian nationalists like Stsiborskyi, international influences like the German 'Conservative Revolution' and the French *Nouvelle Droite*, as well as outright neo-Nazis and advocates of violence and terror. I then discuss, based on these ideological inspirations, what terms we should feel justified in using to describe Azov. I conclude the chapter with a discussion of how these sometimes disparate and contradictory ideologies come together to inform basic core sentiments that underpin the Azov movement.

Ukrainian nationalism: domestic influences

Scroll through enough profiles and posts on social media from people on Ukraine's far right and you'll see the numbers "1044" or "10/44" appear at least a few times. Whether it's tagged on the end of a message or a screen name, it's a code with roots in the decades well before most of those posting it were even born. The "10" is a reference to the OUN's Decalogue—the original version of which instructed members they "should not hesitate to commit the greatest crime if the good of the cause requires it"—while the "44" refers to a subsequent list called the "Rules of Life for the Ukrainian Nationalist"[10], which among others exhorts followers to "do with your

10 *"Ukrayins'kyy natsionalist: zapovidi, prysyaha, prykmety, pravyla zhyttya, pryrechennia"* ("The Ukrainian nationalist: commandments, oaths, signs, rules of life, destiny"), March 12, 2013, https://osvita.ua/vnz/reports/history/35462/.

enemies what is required for the goodness and greatness of Your Nation."

This kind of radical rhetoric and murderous messaging has its roots in Ukrainian nationalist ideologues of the 1920s and 1930s like Dmytro Dontsov. A Marxist-turned-nationalist, by the 1920s Dontsov had begun to subscribe to a form of fanatically militant nationalism, seeing the nation as a collective personality, an organic entity with an equally organic will carried by a national elite (Zaitsev, 2020). In addition to his virulent anti-Semitism Dontsov advocated violence, preaching a theory of "amorality" ("*amoral'nist'*") that justified any act so long as it was for the good of the nation.

In the leadup to World War II, Dontsov managed to have considerable influence on younger, more radical OUN members who were interested in radical action, even while he was at the same time deemed too extreme and "fanatical" (Shkandrij, 2015) for the OUN's leadership. Dontsov left what is now Ukraine in 1939, eventually making his way to Canada where he died in 1973.

Dontsov's name doesn't particularly dominate the Azov movement's communications, but he and his thinking have still clearly had some influence. Andriy Biletsky described Dontsov's work as a "classic" in 2018 (Koshkina, 2018), and the movement's so-called chief ideologue Mykola Kravchenko wrote in December 2020 that Dontsov was part of the "foundation" of Ukrainian nationalism, and one who underpins the "elitist components" of Azov's ideas. Eduard Yurchenko, a longtime far-right ideologue associated with the Azov movement, gave a lecture in 2018 under National Corps' banner arguing that Dontsov was a key figure to help understand "the general crisis of European civilization," one that Ukrainians "have a mission to counter."[11]

One of the stranger contemporaries of Dontsov was Yurii Lypa, a poet and medical doctor who was part of the OUN-UPA. In a 1936 essay called "The Ukrainian Race," Lypa argued that all

11 National Corps, "*U Melitopoli proyshla lektsiia «Dmytro Dontsov: vydatnyy polityk ta ideoloh 20 stolittia»*" ("In Melitopol the lecture "Dmitry Dontsov: an outstanding politician and ideologist of the 20th century", was held"), April 1, 2018, https://nationalcorps.org/u-meltopol-projshla-lekcja-dmitro-doncov-vidatnij-poltik-ta-deolog-20-stolttja/.

Ukrainian women needed to be married and give birth for the good of the Ukrainian nation. In one particularly cringeworthy passage (quoted in Rudling, 2019), Lypa wrote that "the 300 ovulations of every Ukrainian woman, as well as 1,500 ejaculations of every Ukrainian man are the same sort of national resources, as, say, its energy supplies and iron, coal, or oil deposits." To this end, Lypa argued that a dictatorial state needed to set up "sexual courts and tribunals" to regulate Ukrainians' sex lives.

Still, Lypa is someone figures within Azov take at least somewhat seriously. "If we're talking about the classics of Ukrainian nationalism," Biletsky said in a 2018 interview when asked about Dmytro Dontsov, "I'm more sympathetic to Yurii Lypa" (Koshkyna, 2018). For Mother's Day in 2021, Azov's National Corps greeted mothers with a message referencing the sex dictatorship advocate, writing on Telegram that "a woman is the guardian of the family…the basis of the ethnic dominant of the Ukrainian national character."

Another contemporary of Dontsov's, Mykola Stsiborksyi, has had a much stronger influence on the Azov movement. A senior ideologue in the OUN, Stsiborskyi developed the concept he called "natiocracy" (*natsiokratiia*), writing a small book by that name in 1935. In this book Stsiborskyi laid out what Zaitsev (2020) bluntly describes as "a Ukrainian model of totalitarianism with a one-party system" modelled in many ways on Fascist Italy. Stsiborskyi's proposed political system, despite his claims that his ideas were novel and unique, reads more like a riff on Italian Fascism. Stsiborskyi held that capitalist liberal democracy only furthered the interests of competing groups, furthered exploitation and that its talk about liberty and equality were nothing but empty phrases.

Whatever one thinks of his diagnosis, Stsiborskyi's cure was worse. His ideal political system, as he makes clear, is a one-party system where a national elite under a single leader as dictator guides the nation, with an economy under state control in a manner not unlike the syndicalism of Italian Fascism, and where equal rights would not exist. For Stsiborskyi (1935), what mattered was "The nation above all!" He further wrote that, in the pursuit of the "liberation" of Ukraine, "nationalism does not limit itself to "universal" precepts of "justice", mercy and humanism." Some of Stsiborksyi's erstwhile colleagues seemed to have taken this lesson to heart—he was assassinated in 1941 allegedly on orders of Stepan Bandera, having been allied with Bandera's rival Andriy Melnyk.

Stsiborskyi's ideas have a receptive audience in Azov. On what would have been Stsiborskyi's 123rd birthday in March 2021, Andriy Biletsky marked the occasion on his Telegram channel with a post praising the ideas of the long-dead ideologue, but carefully avoiding any phrasing that might hint of Stsiborskyi's own Fascist inspirations. "The main idea of natiocracy," Biletsky wrote, "is to form a political system that would ensure only professional and competent Ukrainians come to power."

In 2019 a publishing house affiliated with the Azov movement—Landmark (*Oriientyr*), co-founded by Kravchenko in 2016—put out an edition of Stsiborksyi's *Natiocracy* emblazoned with the movement's Wolfsangel logo. Azov apparently believed enough in the importance of Stsiborskyi's message that in 2020 a German translation was published by far-right publisher Jungeuropa.

Kravchenko wrote in September 2020 about the German edition's publication:

> "Our opponents often look for the origins of Ukrainian nationalism in European right-wing ideologies, and completely ignore the identity of domestic ideologues. We, the newest Ukrainian nationalists, have never rejected our affinity with European Tradition, but today we're focused on the opposite direction. We have sufficient intellectual potential and we're ready to bring Our Ideas to the outside world, not the other way around."[12]

But does everyone in the Azov movement, particularly those interested in ideological discussions, feel the same way? Many in the movement continue to draw much more if not all their inspiration from sources outside Ukraine. This includes figures like National Corps' international secretary Olena Semenyaka, who has said that Azov's role is to "upgrade [the] ideology of Ukrainian nationalism" (quoted in Zeltits, 2019), and others who take most of

12 Notaky Kruka, "*Ukrayins'ka Natsiokratiia i yevropeys'ki chytachi*" ("Ukrainian natiocracy and European readers"), Telegram, September 2020, https://t.me/NKruk/640.

their cues from a bevy of far-right thinkers with roots not in Ukraine, but in places like Weimar Germany.

The Conservative Revolution and non-Nazi fascisms

The seemingly contradictory term 'Conservative Revolution' was popularized by Armin Mohler, a Swiss man who in 1942 deserted his country's army to join the Waffen SS and was "an unrepentant fascist to the end of his life" (Blamires, 2006).

In his 1950 work *The Conservative Revolution in Germany 1918–1932*, based on his PhD dissertation, Mohler discussed a disparate group of writers and thinkers from interwar Germany. While these men often had little if anything to do with each other, they were united by, among other features, hostility to liberal democracy and equality, a yearning for authoritarianism and a longing for spiritual rebirth in the presence of what they saw as the decadence not only of liberalism and socialism, but mainstream conservatism.

These so-called Conservative Revolutionaries included Ernst von Salomon, who served five years in prison in the 1920s for being part of a successful right-wing plot to assassinate Weimar Germany's foreign minister, as well as historian Moeller van den Bruck, who came up with the term 'Third Reich' yet loathed Hitler after first meeting him in the early 1920s.

Many Conservative Revolutionaries had more than just an ambiguous relationship to Nazism. Influential philosopher Martin Heidegger is perhaps less known for his body of work than for his Nazi ties that dogged him until his death in 1976, while political theorist and committed Nazi Carl Schmitt provided legal justifications for Hitler's seizure of power in 1933.

Idiosyncratic Italian anti-Semite and SS admirer Julius Evola is also included among the list of Conservative Revolutionaries. Evola sought radical spiritual renewal based on what he saw as primordial roots of hierarchy and authority back to the times of the ancient Indo-Europeans. This, for the esoteric Evola, held the key to escaping the perceived decay of the modern world into the decadence of egalitarianism: the 'Kali Yuga,' a Hindu term for the darkest of four cyclical ages. Evola's work has inspired the global far right for decades: Italian far-right terrorists of the 1970s and 1980s saw Evola as a mentor (Goodrick-Clarke, 2002). There's no shortage of praise and promotion of Evola's work in the Azov movement's ranks, to the point where one of the founders of the *Plomin'* (Flame) literature club and publishing house affiliated with Azov opened a bar in Kyiv that had as its centrepiece wall decoration a large portrait of a monocled Evola.

One of the most influential Conservative Revolutionary figures was Ernst Junger. Born in 1895 into a wealthy family, Junger became a soldier in the First World War and filled more than a dozen notebooks with observations and thoughts from the trenches. After the war, where he was wounded seven times, he turned these diaries into the book "Storms of Steel." Through these and other books he wrote in the 1920s, Junger wrote about war as a transcendental experience which brought a person to a higher state of being, closer to the organic order of things now sullied by modern civilization.

Through the 1930s Junger rejected overtures from the Nazis, becoming disillusioned with the Nazis' vulgarity and their vote-clamouring populism after being initially approving of them. Despite this break with the Nazis, Junger maintained what Neaman (2019) calls "his own, in some ways more radical, version of the nationalist revolution: authoritarian and ruthless, but not racist."

For decades after the war until his death in 1998 – including a period where his personal secretary was none other than Armin Mohler – Junger produced a diverse corpus of literature touching on issues related to technology, materialism and culture. This body of work managed to earn him fans across the political spectrum, including from socialist French President Francois Mitterand, though Junger said he never regretted anything he'd written.

But it is Junger's early work glorifying war that, not surprisingly, has been a huge inspiration to Azov. Plomin has published two Ukrainian translations of Junger's work, including "Fire and Blood," a telling of his experiences during the First World War. At a presentation of the translation in December 2018, Andriy Biletsky heaped praise on Junger and stressed the German's importance to Azov's soldiers during the height of war in 2014 and 2015. Biletsky said Junger's writings reinforced that the war in Ukraine's east was not just a war in defence of the country but a transformative opportunity, an occasion for both individual and national rebirth. Junger was, according to Biletsky, someone who "touched the eternal, the superhuman... through the bloody but fantastic experience of war" (National Corps, 2019).

Arguably the most vocal booster of Junger and his contemporaries' work within Azov, however, is Olena Semenyaka. The international secretary of National Corps, Semenyaka is the Azov movement's primary international spokesperson (I discuss her role within the Azov movement more in Chapter 6). Junger is one of Semenyaka's primary intellectual influences, the focus of her academic study as a graduate student in philosophy.

The Conservative Revolution has been portrayed by its far-right fans over the past several decades as an alternative to Nazism. They push the apparent anti-Nazi or at least non-Nazi leanings of its members to the forefront, rightly noting that they were generally less into the crass biological racism and anti-Semitism as the Nazis. Nonetheless, it's been argued that the Conservative Revolutionaries' ultra-nationalism, authoritarianism and overall assault on liberal democracy helped lay the groundwork for Nazism (Griffin, 2008).

Moreover, Conservative Revolutionary objections to the Nazis weren't always for the most principled, moral reasons. These figures, generally from more bourgeois backgrounds, were more simply turned off by the vulgarity and violence of the Nazis, disillusioned with their populism as they came to view Nazism as not so much fundamentally abhorrent in principle but more misguided and misdirected. Post-war and contemporary efforts by Conservative Revolution fans, including those in Ukraine, to promote it as some sort of unsullied alternative to Nazism thus ring out as little more than fascist apologetics, an attempt to sell "non-Nazi fascism" (Feldman, 2011) to a new audience.

Some of the biggest fans of the Conservative Revolution's work after the war were found in France, as a number of far-right figures looked to figures like Junger, Evola and others as a foundation for what they hoped would be a new kind of far-right school of thought in the wake of Nazism—the Nouvelle Droite. From the 1970s onwards it has been a hugely influential way of thinking for the global far right.

The *Nouvelle Droite* and metapolitics

Search the website of Plomin for the Ukrainian transliterations of French names like Alain de Benoist, Dominique Venner and Guillaume Faye. You'll get hit after hit of articles about these men and their works—and translations of their articles and of several of their books—and it'll become clear just how much a school of far-right thought born in 1960s France is important to them in 2020s Ukraine.

In 1968, de Benoist and several dozen others with roots on France's far right formed GRECE, an acronym for "Research and Study Group for European Civilization" that spells out the French word for Greece. The legacy not only of the Nazis, but of the collapse of much of France's colonial empire in the 1950s and 1960s, meant de Benoist and his colleagues needed a new way to do politics if they and their far-right ideas were to gain any currency—jettison open racism, anti-Semitism, and sympathies for Nazism and, at least metaphorically, trade in the jackboots for sweater vests. GRECE soon began laying an intellectual foundation for how far-right movements could succeed in the post-Nazi era, and became known broadly as the Nouvelle Droite (New Right).

Besides de Benoist, who still publishes to this day, another foundational figure for the Nouvelle Droite was Dominique Venner. A former member of the Organisation Armée Secrète (OAS), a far-right terrorist group that tried to prevent Algeria's independence and took some 2,000 lives in the process, Venner served 18 months in jail for being part of the organization. When he was released in 1962 he wrote *Toward a Positive Critique*, a book that became a foundational text for what became the Nouvelle Droite several years later. In this book Venner discussed what he saw as the flaws of the French postwar far right, arguing that they needed to adapt what he saw as the tactics of the left—engage the ideological fight not just on a political level, but on a cultural and intellectual level as well. To that end, Venner argued for the "creation of a single revolutionary and nationalist organization" (Ravndal, 2021), an organization made up of "nationalist militants who would be ready for combat."

Venner died in May 2013. He shot himself in Notre Dame Cathedral in Paris, a note on his body lamenting, among other things, what he called "the crime of the replacement of our people" by Muslims. But in death he continues to have his devotees within the Azov movement; Plomin published a Ukrainian translation of *Toward a Positive Critique* in 2019, along with two other works of his. Back in 2015, on the anniversary of his death, some Azov members held a short memorial ceremony for him in front of the French Embassy in Kyiv.

Another Nouvelle Droite figure with an influence on Azov is Guillaume Faye. In the 1990s, Faye coined the term "archaeofuturism," arguing that European nations needed to return to what he deemed ancient, pagan values, like hierarchy and authority, but at the same time acknowledge and maintain the power of modern technology. "When you read our party program you won't find the word "archaeofuturism,"" National Corps international secretary and onetime member of the party's leadership council Olena Semenyaka told me in 2018, "but in fact we kept it in mind when we explained our theoretic basis."

Unlike most thinkers associated with GRECE, however, Faye chose to be unsubtle in his racism, his work becoming more explicitly so after falling out with de Benoist in the 1980s. In his 2000 book *The Colonization of Europe*, he argued war was necessary to expel Muslims from Europe, which earned him a criminal conviction for inciting racial hatred. Faye, who spoke of his fondness for Vladimir Putin after Russia's intervention in eastern Ukraine, died of cancer in 2019.

Arguably the most influential component of the Nouvelle Droite's thought is the concept of metapolitics. Echoing Venner's earlier appeal to ape what he saw as the tactics of the left, the Nouvelle Droite took the thought of Italian Marxist Antonio Gramsci and flipped it on its head. Gramsci, as Bar-On (2007) outlines, argued that the precondition for any Marxist revolution relied on achieving changes in cultural and social consciousness—achieving 'cultural hegemony'—that would open the door longer-term political changes. Applying this to the far right, de Benoist and his colleagues at GRECE argued that, if their ideas were to have any hope of becoming dominant in a world they felt was conquered by the left—especially in the wake of World War II and what Dan Stone (2014) refers to as the "anti-fascist consensus" in Europe—they needed to slowly create the right cultural and intellectual conditions before they could even think about real, lasting political power. This included engaging in key elites in media, academia, the education system, literary circles and beyond to, as Bar-On (2013) phrases it, capture the "laboratories of thought."

There is, of course, much more to the Nouvelle Droite's thought than just archaeofuturism or metapolitics. The Nouvelle Droite promotes a vision of an ideal world of hierarchy and order, one of ethnically homogeneous nations with an ostensible 'right to difference' from others. Its thinkers thus reject equality, multiculturalism and non-European immigration to Europe. Thinkers like de Benoist look back to Europe's pagan Indo-European roots for inspiration, and see a model of hierarchy in the ancients that has been polluted by both Judaism and Christianity—dominant religions and modes of thought that, in their view, have pushed an artificial egalitarianism onto the world. The Nouvelle Droite also pushes an anti-capitalist and nominally anti-imperialist message—another borrowing from the left—arguing that capitalism eradicates national differences and subsumes them into a bland, homogenous pan-national cocktail. The answer for the Nouvelle Droite is, of course, not socialism but rather a market constrained by national forces, by a learned elite acting in the best interests of the ethnic group or nation (Bar-On, 2013).

Whether Azov as a whole has been directly influenced by the Nouvelle Droite is debatable. However, as I make clear in Chapter 5 of this book, the concept of metapolitics, whether consciously or not, underpins much of how the Azov movement acts, communicates and presents itself in Ukraine and beyond.

Is the concept of metapolitics itself dangerous? After all, those who practice it wear their non-violent bona fides on their sleeves, and act just as ready for a reasoned debate as anyone else. But those who practice metapolitics are doing so while waiting for the right time for a far-right revolution to overthrow liberal democracy. Worse, some on the global far right seem to easily lose patience with metapolitics. These impatient extremists have sometimes opted for "more militant forms of activism, including terrorism" (Ravndal, 2021), with a key example being the 1970s Ordine Nuovo (New Order) in Italy—ironically, a group who some within Azov have written about positively and promoted, as I discuss below.

Even if they sometimes take part in what seem to be the trappings of metapolitics, some within the Azov movement say and do things that would probably make most Nouvelle Droite thinkers shake their heads—wearing racism, anti-Semitism, Nazi sympathies and love of violence and terrorism on their sleeves as a source of pride.

Neo-Nazism, violence and terror

"Fuhrernacht," as the name might suggest, was a 2019 spectacle so over the top you could be forgiven for thinking it was a bad joke.

On the night of April 30, 2019—74 years to the day after Adolf Hitler killed himself in his bunker in Berlin—the neo-Nazi network Wotanjugend hosted a private night of Hitler worship in Kyiv. Wotanjugend, with roots in Russia but now based in Ukraine, is largely led by Russian neo-Nazi, Azov Regiment veteran and Kyiv resident Alexey Levkin.

In a now-deleted post on Wotanjugend's website[13], Hitler is referred to as "a fire whose tongues bring light to heroes and death to enemies." Several neo-Nazi bands, to a select few dozen attendees, played songs around a framed photo of Hitler surrounded by candles, Celtic crosses and flags bearing a Black Sun, a neo-Nazi symbol used by Azov movement since its beginnings. The night was capped off with a performance by one of Levkin's bands—Adolfkvlt, a band devoted to "esoteric Hitlerism," Wotanjugend's

13 The article was removed from the website at some point after I wrote about Wotanjugend and "Fuhrernacht" for Bellingcat in September 2019. An archived version of the Wotanjugend article can be found at https://archive.is/hKRzT.

website described in the now-deleted post, "the cult of which came to life on this mysterious evening."

Esoteric Hitlerism, or esoteric Nazism, is a bizarre set of mystical beliefs held by some neo-Nazis. Inspirations for these beliefs include Savitri Devi, a French-born Nazi occultist and Hindu who saw Hitler as an incarnation of the god Vishnu, and Miguel Serrano, a Chilean who believed that Hitler survived the war to live in a secret base with alien gods under the Antarctic ice sheet, a base from which he would someday emerge with a fleet of UFOs to lead humanity out of the Kali Yuga. Devi and Serrano's works have been referenced and promoted on Wotanjugend's social media.

There are some within Azov movement and related subgroups that subscribe to open neo-Nazism, including Wotanjugend and NordStorm, a small Kharkiv-based neo-Nazi group that takes part in events alongside Wotanjugend and Azov's Centuria organization. These groups continue to publish unapologetic Nazi-inspired rhetoric including open anti-Semitism, encourage violence and praise Hitler and other Nazis. While it's unclear the extent to which these kinds types of beliefs are common across the entire Azov movement, it's clear at the very least that there is a vocal minority of individuals within it who are neo-Nazis.

Unlike some of the other ideological inspirations I've discussed above, these neo-Nazis generally don't even try to engage in the trappings of intellectual sophistication or clever presentation of their ideas. They sprinkle their neo-Nazi rhetoric with doses of Julius Evola's radical traditionalism, drawing on his thoughts about perceived European decay and ancient, apparently eternal truths about hierarchy and authority. They stress Ukraine's Indo-European past, especially perceived warriors like the Scythians, to present Ukraine as a sort of true European homeland, one where these purported ancient values reigned. They take the notion of a so-called 'great replacement,' an anti-Semitic conspiracy theory that there is a plan by elites to replace white Europeans by non-whites, particularly Muslims, and use it to openly justify violence.

While the leadership of the Azov movement today does not communicate open anti-Semitism or openly neo-Nazi rhetoric—something which I will discuss more in Chapter 5 of this book—the movement's roots are in exactly that. Biletsky has a history of involvement in explicitly anti-Semitic organizations and using openly anti-Semitic, racist rhetoric, writing about the need to "cleanse" Ukraine of foreigners in a 2013 pamphlet of his writings called *Word of the White Leader*. The hagiographic preface of this work, written by comrades of Biletsky, references a "long-dead German"—an obvious reference to Adolf Hitler—who outlined the qualities of a successful leader, qualities Biletsky apparently also possessed. "We have not changed," Biletsky said in October 2014. "Azov's heart is based on its right-wing ideology. It's the legacy of Patriot of Ukraine" (quoted in Reporting Radicalism, 2021).

These neo-Nazis, as well as others within the Azov movement, have plenty of positive things to say about authors who explicitly justify violence or have even taken part in such violence themselves. These include figures like Romanian interwar far-right leader Corneliu Codreanu, an obsessive anti-Semite and leader of the Iron Guard who served a prison sentence for murder in the 1920s and told his followers that violence was necessary to redeem Romania. Since 2020, Ukrainian readers can learn about Codreanu and the Iron Guard thanks to a Plomin translation of a number of selections of Iron Guard thinkers, including excerpts from Codreanu himself. They also include figures like American white nationalist Greg Johnson, who despite being an advocate of a metapolitical strategy is considered one of the few contemporary far-right intellectuals with sympathies for Nazism (Sedgwick, 2019). Johnson, who has advocated ethnic cleansing in his writings (2014) and is openly anti-Semitic, was a guest of the Azov movement at a 2019 conference in Kyiv, where he distributed copies of his newest book.

Elements within the Azov movement also have good things to say about far-right terrorists. Wotanjugend has referred to Anders Breivik, who killed 77 people in the 2006 Norway terror attacks, and Timothy McVeigh, perpetrator of the 1995 Oklahoma City attacks that killed 168 people, as "heroes" (Bellingcat Anti-Equality Monitoring, 2019). In 2019 Plomin published a translation of a work by Italian far-right terrorist Franco Freda, who was deemed by an Italian court in 2004 to have been partly responsible for a far-right terror attack in 1969 that killed 17 people. This came after they also published a translation of a book by Pierluigi Concutelli, an Italian neo-fascist terrorist convicted of murder.

These same elements within Azov also spoke positively of Brenton Tarrant, the perpetrator of the Christchurch terror attacks that took 51 lives. Some even promoted translations of his infamous manifesto. Wotanjugend published a Russian-language translation on their website in March 2019; the livestreamed video of the attacks was also published on Wotanjugend's Telegram channel (both the translated manifesto and the video have since been deleted). Karpatska Sich, a far-right group in the western city of Uzhhorod that has a relationship with the Azov movement, encouraged its members to buy a Ukrainian translation of the manifesto in August 2019, a post that has also since been deleted. In the wake of the Christchurch attacks Yevhen Vriadnyk, an Azov veteran who co-founded Plomin, defended Tarrant's actions on his own Telegram channel, calling it "revenge" for a so-called "genocide of Europeans." While most of these posts about the Christchurch terrorist have since been deleted, Vriadnyk's remained online as of autumn 2021.

On its face, this sort of neo-Nazism and open advocacy of violence clashes with other ideological influences, particularly those who draw inspiration from a more metapolitical approach. Within Azov it certainly does clash in some way, but more in the sense of optics and public relations than in terms of any sort of ideological incoherence. At some point after September 2019—and despite the two working together in the past—Semenyaka reportedly fell out with Levkin over his open and "too provocative" neo-Nazi activism that "gave bad publicity to Semenyaka's ambitions" (Nonjon, 2020).

But there isn't quite the hard border separating those within the movement who are smart enough to disavow, or honestly do not believe in, outright neo-Nazism and violence. The core common beliefs across Azov certainly differ in their intensity and the means with which they're expressed. However, across whatever narrow ideological divides that exist within the movement, they are still more similar than different.

What do we call Azov?

Scholars usually use one of two terms to refer to groups or individuals on the far right: 'radical right' (sometimes itself used in place of the term 'far right') and 'extreme right'. Looking at how these terms are defined, using the term 'extreme' (i.e., 'far-right extremist') is more than justified in the context of the Azov movement.

The radical right, as Ravndal (2021) observes, accepts some form of democracy, "just not the liberal version" – they are generally disinterested in liberal democratic principles like minority rights. The radical right accepts at least procedural democracy (Halikiopolou, 2018) and downplays or denies links to fascism and the far right. These primarily include political parties that have seen electoral success in western Europe, like the Alternative for Germany (AfD), France's Rassemblement National (formerly the Front National) and Austria's Freedom Party (FPÖ).

What differentiates the extreme right from the radical right, for most scholars, are their views on democracy and violence. Those on the far right who explicitly reject democracy and favour violence and "other unconventional methods to promote their alternative worldview" are extreme right rather than radical right (Ravndal, 2021). Those on the extreme right explicitly "seek the overthrow of liberal democracy" (Eatwell, 2003) even if, like the Azov movement with its National Corps political party, they also take part in elections. Unlike the radical right, those on the extreme right have much more transparent links to fascism and fascist-inspired ideologies (Halikiopolou, 2018) and justify some degree of violence in pursuit of its aims (Jupskås and Segers, 2020). Based on this definition, it's clear that the Azov movement, with its ideologues' praise of dictatorship, ideological disdain for democracy and justification and glorification of political violence, can be called a far-right extremist movement.

Up to this point I've used 'far right' as a general term to describe the movement, and will continue to do so throughout this book. But there's another f-word that we should feel okay using to describe overarching Azov's ideology, one that helps us understand more of what they represent to the core – fascism.

There's no doubt that accusing someone of fascism or calling someone a 'fascist' is a tired term of abuse—least of all in Ukraine, where it carries a certain amount of baggage thanks to its (over)use in Soviet and subsequent Russian propaganda. Still, it's worth reviewing some of the definitions of fascism from academic literature, given that there's a particularly extensive literature on the subject.

A relatively simple and straightforward definition comes from Kevin Passmore (2002), who describes fascism as "a set of ideologies and practices that seeks to place the nation, defined in exclusive biological, cultural, and/or historical terms, above all other sources of loyalty, and to create a mobilized national community." It's hard not to see outlines of Azov in this definition, particularly in the way that the nation is the highest priority—like in the "Ukraine above all!" slogan for National Corps and partners' 2019 parliamentary election campaign—and how Azov, as I will discuss, tries to mobilize its followers into action.

Some of most-discussed definitions of fascism are a touch unwieldy, but they're important to think about. British historian Roger Griffin defined fascism as "palingenetic ultranationalism" (1991), seeing it as a kind of politics seeking national rebirth through a revolution against liberal democracy, liberalism, conservatism socialism, a revolution premised on presumed unchanging ancient values. Griffin (2002) further explained that fascism is "extremely heterogeneous in the specific ideology of its many permutations," but still revolves around the notion that rebirth and liberation from "a period of perceived decadence and degeneracy."

There are even stronger outlines of Azov visible in Griffin's definition and discussions of fascism. Consider, in 2019, Olena Semenyaka describing Azov's National Corps to an international audience as the only force that could make a revitalized Ukrainian nationalism "a basis for the national rebirth led by the patriotic war generation" (quoted in Zeltits, 2019). Consider in 2015 when a "March of Rebirth" was held in the city of Zhytomyr and described as "the beginning of the blossoming of the Ukrainian Nation, the beginning of the struggle, the purpose of which is the reconstruction and exaltation of the Ukrainian State" (Reporter, 2015). At the core here is the idea of a rebirth of a decayed Ukraine—and indeed of all of Europe—through an anti-liberal, anti-egalitarian, anti-democratic revolution.

American historian of fascism Robert Paxton (2004) has an observation about fascism that must be considered, particularly when discussing ideologies and inspirations: fascism is fundamentally more about emotional appeal than any profound intellectual program. He warns that, in trying to understand fascism is, that to "focus only on the educated carriers of intellect and culture in the search for fascist roots…is to miss the most important register: subterranean passions and emotions." While its purported ideologues have tried to do so over the years, fascism doesn't have the sort of systematic intellectual foundations that, for example, liberal, socialism, communism or even mainstream conservatism have (Paxton, 2004).

If anything, there's something profoundly anti-intellectual in much of what fascist ideologues preach, whether Dontsov's amorality or Evola's esoteric knowledge of apparently eternal, unchanging truths. This seems especially the case with the Azov movement, where its purported intellectual foundations often seem like a house made on sand, assembled from pieces of decades-old driftwood and marketed as a hot new property.

Still, it's important to understand Azov's ideologies and its inspirations, to understand the thinking that guides those within movement, from its leadership to its linked smaller subgroups that I discuss in the following chapter. In addition, it's critical to understand how these relatively disparate ideologies and inspirations come together into common core sentiments, and how they motivate the movement.

Azov's core sentiments

Below are a set of what I call the common core sentiments of the Azov movement. What may well strike the reader is that these core sentiments aren't new, and certainly aren't revelatory to anyone familiar with historical fascism or contemporary far-right movements. What I've outlined briefly below can describe, in various ways, the feelings about politics, society and the world around them that underpin a number of similar far-right movements across the globe.

The first of these core sentiments is a belief in *hierarchy*. Whether they take their inspiration from Mykola Stsiborskyi, Ernst Junger, Alain de Benoist, Greg Johnson or anyone in between, society should be set up in a hierarchical fashion, with those perceived as strongest and most naturally able to lead at the top. Equality is a myth and a society that isn't set up hierarchically, that doesn't put the 'best' at the top to lead in effect rewards the unworthy and punishes the worthy.

Related to this is a focus on *elitism* and *authority*. As Azov's chief ideologue Mykola Kravchenko wrote on his Telegram channel in January 2021, dictatorship isn't a bad thing if it's done right—'right', of course, meaning a dictator who "will take full responsibility for the fate of the Nation," in Kravchenko's words.[14] Those who should lead and guide the nation are born, not made, and their authority is not to be questioned or challenged. Liberal concepts like minority rights or checks and balances are to be rejected.

Tradition is paramount, but not in the sense that mainstream conservatives might believe. Tradition isn't folk embroidery or old recipes, or even wanting things to be the way one feels they were decades ago; tradition, rather, is treated as an ancient, unchanging and unyielding force, embodied in hierarchy and authority and order, that must be (re)captured and brought to life in a modern society still bearing all the futuristic-seeming advances of the early 21st century—an alternative modernity.

The nation (or capital-N 'Nation,' as seen in some Azov writings) is *organic*. Ukrainian "ethno-cultural identity," Olena Semenyaka told a Portuguese far-right group in 2019, is itself an "organic life form" that needs to be saved from the west's decline. For leader Biletsky (zik, 2017), "nationalism is zero percent selfishness. It's when you feel part of something bigger and are willing to sacrifice your freedom and, sometimes, your health for the sake of a larger community, a nation..." That which prioritizes any interest

---

14 Notaky Kruka, "*Chy mozhe dyktatura buty blahom?*" ("Can dictatorship be a good thing?"), Telegram, January 16, 2021, https://t.me/NKruk/973.

other than the nation, like gender or sexual orientation, is a problem. As Biletsky himself stated in 2019, "if it fights against the Ukrainian idea, which is embodied in practice in so many respects by Azov and National Corps, then it is the enemy!" (Polishchuk and Suvorov, 2019).

There is a paranoid fixation on *conspiracies*, a feeling that there are coordinated plots against them, whether large or small or from east or west. Whether it's international criticism coming from authors like myself, domestic criticism coming from civil society groups or invective coming from Russian state media, nothing is ever accidental. Exactly who's behind the conspiracies can differ—the Kremlin, Ukrainian politicians, western liberals, 'globalists' (i.e., Jews) and so on—but Azov, in their view, are beset by foes and plotters on all sides scheming to bring them and the country down.

Rebirth on a national level, not just an individual level, is fundamental. The 2014 revolution and Russia's military intervention in eastern Ukraine provided the opportunity for wholescale national rebirth, a rebirth in perceived ancient values—a rebirth in which Azov sees itself as the vanguard. War is a perfect opportunity for this rebirth—an opportunity, per Biletsky speaking about Junger in 2019, to touch the eternal, the superhuman.

Part of this process of rebirth comes through *violence*. This, of course, operates on one hand through the experience of war, but it also operates in the form of extralegal political violence against perceived internal enemies, whether they be purportedly traitorous former Azov figures, alleged pro-Russians, local leftists, or western-backed LGBT+ activists. Regardless of form, however, violence in the name of redeeming the nation is worthy of praise—and, when necessary to present a more palatable picture to a mainstream audience, framed as self-defence or simply downplayed and denied to be 'violence' at all.

Lastly, a belief in *victimhood*—and a corresponding justification to take action, including violence, against the apparent victimizers and their accomplices—underpins much of how the global far right operates, but does so particularly strongly in Ukraine. The country has been the target of military intervention by a former colonial power for almost eight years, so it's not hard for a Ukrainian of any political stripe to feel like a victim. Ukraine, in their view, has forever been the victim not only of a more powerful neighbour that they see as their historical enemy and perpetual obstacle to real independence, but also the victim of western nations too ready to sacrifice Ukraine and too scared to confront Russia. This, of course, isn't necessarily a sentiment unique to the far right, and it's not one without at least some justification. But for Azov, that sense of victimization goes deeper, and justifies extreme action in the name of the capital-N Nation.

Still, as one reviews Azov's ideologies and its inspirations, it's important not to fall into the trap of assuming that what a political actor states and writes, least of all on the far right, is always indicative of how they will act. In other words, it's important to look not just what Azov says, but what it does and how it does it—the subject of the following chapter.

Chapter 3: Azov in Action

They marched past as I stood there on Khreshchatyk, Kyiv's sprawling main thoroughfare, with my camera in my hands and, given the times, a mask over my mouth and nose.

It was August 24, 2020: Independence Day. I was watching the second March of the Defenders of Ukraine, an event organized by a broad coalition of veterans and activists that included the far right. After being elected president of Ukraine in 2019, Volodymyr Zelenskyy cancelled what was until the previous year an annual state-funded military parade. The chief organizer of the march was Dmytro Shatrovskyi, an Azov Regiment veteran and head of the Azov-affiliated Veterans Brotherhood.

I saw Centuria first, a group that hadn't even existed a month earlier. I snapped photos of the hundred or so mostly teenagers in their matching black t-shirts and black face masks. One of the column's leaders was a hulking, heavily tattooed figure, someone I'd later learn was also a leader of an openly neo-Nazi group.

Behind them was a group of a few hundred National Corps activists, a mix of teenagers up front and older folks in behind, all in grey branded t-shirts and carrying banners at the front that read "We support the Azov Regiment." Maybe a dozen young women, clad in black and each holding a single rose, marched behind them with a banner that read "Azov dismantles Russian positions, not women's hearts." They were members of a small Azov-affiliated women's group that would itself be basically discarded and forgotten within a few months.

Less than five minutes behind them, after small columns of veterans of unrelated military units, marched the Azov Regiment itself. Several hundred veterans and supporters, shrouded in smoke from flares, carried flags bearing the Regiment's Wolfsangel logo. The column was led by Andriy Biletsky, who relinquished command of the Regiment in 2016, with Maksym Zhorin at his side, who took over command until he himself relinquished it in 2017. Almost all were in military uniform from the waist down, wearing matching brown t-shirts with "Ukraine above all!" printed on the back. As they and other marchers got to Maidan, a huge banner had been draped over the glass façade of the shopping mall on Maidan to greet them. "Azov wishes you a happy Independence Day"("*Azov vitaie z Dnem nezalezhnosti!*"), it read, again bearing Azov's logo. The march, in total, drew an estimated 50,000 attendees.

Watching Azov in action here provided, at least in part, a picture of how the movement is organized and how it functions. Biletsky had a role leading a Regiment on one its biggest parades of the year, a Regiment he hadn't led in five years. As one affiliated subgroup rebranded just weeks before the march, another disappeared within a few months with no official reason why. Veterans I recognized in the Regiment's column were ones I knew were also affiliated with other extreme subgroups. And it all taking place a dash away from the Azov movement's three-story social centre nestled up a side street from the square.

Still, this was only a quick glance at the movement. In this chapter I focus on what the Azov movement is, what it consists of and, critically, what the movement's parts actually do in practice. Azov is a fluid, heterogeneous movement, a movement where observers don't always agree on what even comprises it. To try and provide some clarity, I present in this chapter an overview of different elements of the Azov movement, what they do and, generally speaking, how they relate to each other.

The Azov movement: an overview

International observers, whether academics, government officials or other journalists, still too often talk about the entire Azov movement as just the 'Battalion.' They forget or, in some cases, simply don't know that there's much more to Azov than just the military unit that gave the movement its name. Most media coverage that discusses the movement (including much of my own, in fairness) focuses primarily on central elements, including personalities like Andriy Biletsky, the National Corps political party or, before it was rebranded in 2020, the National Militia street force.

But there's much more than that. As the movement's main international representative Olena Semenyaka told me at Azov's Cossack House in December 2018:

> "We probably have now about 45 different projects that we constantly develop. All of them have coordinators, so all of them have coordinator criteria to estimate their success... so if they don't meet the demands the managers are changed, altered, of course, it's quite serious. This is our way to create a state within the state."

This statement underscores not only that Azov is a much broader movement than is sometimes thought at first glance, but it's a movement constantly in flux. It's a movement where relatively high-profile individual figures within it can rise and fall in prominence over just a few months. New initiatives sprout up suddenly while others fade away with barely a word. The movement's public campaigning and activism on a specific issue can end just as suddenly as it began.

One way I've tried to explain the Azov movement as a whole to people, including all its related subgroups, organizations and initiatives, is to begin by imagining it as a giant umbrella. Underneath the core of the umbrella, holding it up, are the Azov Regiment, National Corps and, to a lesser degree, Centuria. This core holds up the roof for groups – those officially affiliated, unofficially affiliated and nominally independent organizations – to function with varying degrees of autonomy and affiliation to the Azov movement.

Next furthest out from the core are groups like Youth Corps, Sports Corps and Veterans Brotherhood. These are groups and initiatives that have a degree of official affiliation with Azov, which can include, for example, using Azov branding or being promoted by senior leaders of the movement. Some of these initiatives are explicitly noted as initiatives of National Corps and use the party's branding and logo.

Further out are groups and initiatives that don't necessarily have an open, 'official' affiliation with Azov, like Wotanjugend, but still clearly function as part of the movement; its members are part of other groups within the movement, including National Corps. These include small initiatives of individual activists, as well as tactical training organizations run by Azov Regiment veterans or by others with relationships to the Azov movement.

Furthest out under this roof are independent organizations that nonetheless have strong relationships with the Azov movement, like Tradition and Order or Freikorps. Beyond them are organizations like C14 (now called Foundation for the Future, *Osnova maybutnoho*), organizations that exist outside of Azov and have conflicted in the past but now occasionally cooperate with them.

The core: Azov Regiment, National Corps and Centuria

The Azov Regiment—officially the Special Operations Detachment 'Azov'—is part of Ukraine's National Guard, a gendarmerie under the authority of Ukraine's interior ministry. The ministry was led from February 2014, right after the revolution, until July 2021 by Arsen Avakov. Despite it sometimes being casually referred to as the "Azov Battalion" in English, the Regiment hasn't been a battalion proper since September 2014.

After being pulled from the frontlines in August 2015 along with other volunteer units, the Regiment went back to the front in February 2019, where it continues to fight today. The Regiment is home to approximately 1,000 soldiers serving at a time, with a few thousand veterans of the Regiment across Ukraine and beyond.

Even as the war ebbs and flows in intensity, with the Regiment seldom if ever taking part in the kinds of bloody battles seen in 2014 and 2015, the Regiment and the wider movement play up its success as a fighting force. Its defenders promote it as the strongest detachment within Ukraine's military, using "appealing self-marketing" (Gomza and Zajaczkowski, 2019) to give it and the wider movement a significant measure of social and political capital in Ukraine which I discuss later in this book.

The ideological orientations of those who fight and have fought within the Regiment isn't always as clear-cut as assumed, though the Regiment's leaders have roots in Ukraine's far right. In 2015, one representative of the Regiment claimed between 10 to 20 percent of the unit were neo-Nazis (Dorrell, 2015). A number of foreign fighters with far-right views have served in the unit, primarily neo-Nazis from Russia like Sergei Korotkikh or Wotanjugend's Alexey Levkin, but also fighters from places like Sweden and Croatia. There reportedly has been at least some degree of indoctrination of far-right ideas in the Regiment; there have been reported cases (Likhachev, 2018b) of young men, seemingly apolitical, entered the Regiment and within six months becoming neo-Nazis. The Regiment and the broader movement, however, continue to reject any associations of the unit with the far right, particularly when far-right extremism and terrorism are mentioned.

Unlike the rest of the Azov movement, the Regiment functions under different legal authority as part of Ukraine's interior ministry. Still, it would be a mistake to claim because of this that the Azov Regiment is somehow not part of the broader Azov movement. Biletsky, the self-described leader of the entire movement, is still treated and greeted as a leader at the Regiment. As Kuzmenko (2020) notes, the Regiment welcomes National Corps activists and leaders at its bases, has shot campaign videos with the Regiment and sees its recruitment efforts promoted by Azov movement figures. The Regiment's recruitment base at ATEK, a disused factory on the outskirts of Kyiv, is also a home for numerous Azov events, including a 'gathering of the Azov movement' in August 2020. Moreover, the Regiment has been explicitly described as the "military wing" of the Azov movement by Olena Semenyaka on numerous occasions, including at least four times to international audiences in 2019 alone.

"What do we need now?" Andriy Biletsky asked a crowd in a Kyiv meeting hall on October 14, 2016. "A good party platform? A hundred broadcasts and debates? Ukraine's fed up with that."

"We have to become a party of real action," Biletsky continued. "Nothing but action. No words, billboards, spending time on TV shows, debates or anything like that."

Biletsky was speaking at the founding session of the Azov movement's political party, National Corps. The date Azov chose for the party's founding congress was no coincidence—the mythical founding date of the UPA. Biletsky was chosen as party leader by the assembled delegates by a reported vote of 292 to 0 as Nazariy

Kravchenko, an Azov Regiment veteran and member of Ukraine's football ultras subculture, became the party's first deputy chair.

As a political party, National Corps has been an absolute dud at the ballot box. After being nominated by the party, Biletsky ended up pulling out of 2019's presidential elections months before the vote, with one poll in December 2018 showing him in 20th place with an embarrassing 0.2 percent of the potential vote. A few months later in parliamentary elections, a coalition between National Corps and other far-right organizations could muster barely 2 percent of the vote, nowhere near the 5 percent threshold needed to enter Ukraine's parliament. After local elections in October 2020, National Corps managed to elect two dozen representatives across the country in local assemblies—perhaps a bit more impressive-sounding at first but less so when you realize it's a mere two dozen of the more than 40,000 in total that were elected across the country.

Electoral failures aside, National Corps has become the primary public-facing body of the entire Azov movement. The party is marketed in such a way as to be more acceptable for mainstream public consumption; far-right symbols like the Wolfsangel logo, for example, aren't part of its public imagery (Reporting Radicalism, 2021). Regardless, the U.S. Department of State referred to National Corps as a "nationalist hate group" in 2019.[15]

National Corps' language in its public communications is polished, precise and seldom betrays a hint of having come from a far-right party. This communication itself is, for lack of a better word, slick—the party promotes its actions with professional-quality photography and sometimes equally high quality, well-edited video clips. National Corps representatives have appeared on Ukrainian television channels—including frequently on channels connected to Putin friend Viktor Medvedchuk before these channels were banned in February 2021. Aside from Biletsky, National Corps representatives on television have included head of the party's central

---

15 United States Department of State, "Ukraine 2018 Human Rights Report," https://www.state.gov/wp-content/uploads/2019/03/UKRAINE-2018-HUMAN-RIGHTS-REPORT.pdf.

headquarters Maksym Zhorin, Kyiv branch leader Serhiy Tamarin and Sergei Korotkikh.

National Corps has claimed to have approximately 10,000 members (cf. Miller, 2018) though other observers have estimated lower figures, some as low as 6,500 members.[16] The party's activists and those who take part in its events are often young people; it's not uncommon to be at National Corps events, as I have, and be struck by the number of teenagers in attendance, usually young men, wearing branded National Corps jackets or t-shirts. Some of these activists, as discussed below, are also active in other Azov-related subgroups, some of which are more openly extreme in their views.

National Corps' social media pages, particularly Telegram, and its own website seldom go more than a few days without promoting some action party members have held somewhere. These include protests and demonstrations – like those held against then-president Petro Poroshenko in advance of presidential elections 2019, or violent protests against a proposed land reform bill later that year – commemorations like an annual torchlit march honouring the birth of Stepan Bandera, as well as pickets and sometimes vandalism of businesses they claim are doing business with Russia. In 2021 National Corps' activities also included organizing what it called 'civil defense' events, holding an open event called 'Let's Defend Ukraine!' where basic combat and tactical training was provided (Rekawek, 2021).

The party has claimed that it is primarily funded by membership fees. This has been called into question, and the party appears to have other undisclosed sources of funding (Feshchenko et al, 2020). In addition, National Corps members have themselves been paid by the party to appear at events (Spirin, 2019).

---

16 Cf. Rosa Luxemburg Foundation in Ukraine, "*Konfrontatsiyi ta nasyl'stvo ul'trapravykh v Ukrayini 14.10.2018-14.10.2019*" ("Far-right confrontations and violence in Ukraine, 14.10.2018-14.10.2019"), January 18, 2020, http://rosalux.org.ua/ua/publications/196-ultra-right-violence-monitoring-2018-2019.

For years in Ukraine, members of far-right groups have acted as thugs-for-hire for powerful figures in Ukrainian society: politicians, oligarchs and other business magnates looking to protect their interests and squeeze out competitors, and willing to pay far-right hooligans as muscle to help them do so (Likhachev, 2018). Azov's predecessor Patriot of Ukraine took part in this very activity in Kharkiv for allies of Arsen Avakov in the 2000s. Today, members of National Corps have also been accused of being part of this trend of *reiderstvo* – a Russian word common across the post-Soviet space referring to when business owners, benefiting from weak rule of law, use dubious if not outright fraudulent means to try and take over companies and properties. Since 2016 members of National Corps are alleged to have raided and seized properties, instigated protests and intimidated competitors at the behest of powerful interests, some of which I discuss in more detail in Chapter 4.

National Corps members have taken part in a considerable number of acts of political violence over the years, carrying out physical attacks on their perceived enemies, from LGBT+ Ukrainians and left-wing activists to perceived pro-Russians (Gorbach, 2018). In August 2020 National Corps members physically attacked members of perceived pro-Russian political forces numerous times, including an attack on a minibus that involved multiple National Corps representatives being detained for several months awaiting charges (the cases are still pending as of late 2021). While National Corps denied involvement, the party nonetheless defended the attackers as 'patriots', with Biletsky even visiting some of the defendants in court.

Some of those detained in August 2020 were former members of the National Militia. Founded in 2018, the National Militia (*Natsionalni druzhyny*) was founded to function as a street paramilitary force, ostensibly to help maintain law and order in Ukraine's streets. Ihor Mykhailenko, an Azov Regiment veteran and member of Azov's predecessor organization Patriot of Ukraine, was its founder. Mykhailenko has been alleged to have been involved in a 2016 armed robbery along with other Azov veterans (Furmaniuk, 2016); Mykhailenko has denied any involvement (Hlukohavskyi and Hruzdiev, 2018).

National Militia's few thousand young, mostly male members became noticeable for their ubiquitous blue camouflaged jackets that some commentators noted bore a resemblance to the former units of the Berkut riot police, disbanded after the revolution in 2014. These jackets, as Mykhailenko himself noted (Hlukohavskyi and Hruzdiev, 2018), cost each National Militia members up to 700 hryvnia each, approximately US$25.

But National Militia soon became noticeable for other reasons. Observers in domestic and international media worried that the ambitious National Militia, which said it "will not hesitate to use force to establish order" (quoted in Miller, 2018), would try to act as a vigilante force outside of state control. While Azov figures and even Arsen Avakov himself tried to quell these concerns, National Militia members didn't help by, among other things, intimidating elected officials in council meetings and attacking a Roma camp within the first six months of 2018. Like National Corps, National Militia also took part in so-called 'raids' of markets and the like, allegedly for business or political patrons (cf. Fraza, 2018).

These concerns carried over into 2019, when Ukraine's Central Election Commission gave permission to the National Militia to officially monitor Ukraine's presidential elections. "If we need to punch someone in the face in the name of justice," Mykhailenko wrote on Telegram in advance of the vote, "we will do so without hesitation." These concerns led G7 countries to send a letter to Avakov (Miller, 2019), urging him to prevent election-related violence from "extreme political movements" like National Militia, who at the time were involved in a number of violent confrontations with police at protests against then-president Petro Poroshenko. In the end, likely owing at least somewhat to this pressure and unwanted international attention, the elections passed with no incidents from the National Militia.

But they wouldn't be around too much longer. In April 2020, in the midst of the beginning of the COVID-19 pandemic, Mykhailenko spoke with Kyiv National Corps leader Serhiy Tamarin about the troubles he and his brethren had in motivating youth, essentially admitting that there was some degree of stagnation and lack of excitement from youth in the movement in what they were doing.

"Maybe it makes sense to wait for the revanche [of pro-Russian forces] that everyone keeps talking about," Mykhailenko said in the since-deleted YouTube video. "It might push youth towards some deed because, in my opinion, the youth feels the need to act only when there's something to overcome."

A few months after that video National Militia disappeared and Centuria emerged, quite literally, from the dark. On the night of July 31, 2020, a nighttime ceremony with torches, matching black shirts, chants in unison and a gun salute was held outside Kyiv. There Mykhailenko led the few hundred assembled Centuria members—some of whom, one source claimed (Chepurko, 2020), were also National Corps activists— into the world.

"Disciplined, organized and determined: ready to fight any enemy of Ukraine," Mykhailenko wrote afterwards on his Telegram channel. "Everything…anti-Ukrainian will be destroyed!" Centuria's official new Telegram channel added a few days later that "we reserve the right to use any methods and techniques" to combat the so-called "fifth column" in Ukraine. This came months ahead of local elections in Ukraine, as the Azov movement focused its energies on attacking perceived pro-Russian political foes, primarily popular Spain-based blogger Anatoliy Shariy—a man loathed by many pro-western Ukrainians—and the small party he had formed around himself.

With its use of ancient Roman imagery, focus on ritual and its glorification of war and cleansing the country of enemies, Centuria presents itself as an elite club slowly preparing for battle. To that end, Centuria's focus is less on the streets—though they do take part in protests and other actions—and instead mostly on combat and tactical training, even taking part in knife fight training sessions and tournaments. Centuria also has what it calls Legionnaires, "the most devoted members" of the movement. Azov ideologist Mykola Kravchenko wrote of Centuria's 'initiation' ritual of these Legionnaires on Telegram in December 2020, talking about the event as an initiation into a sacred, ancient band of warriors, with each member someone who serves the Ukrainian nation.

Centuria appears to be linked to two explicitly neo-Nazi groups I discuss in more detail below, NordStorm and Wotanjugend. This extremism was on full display in September 2021: in a post on their Telegram channel showing off a firearms training session, Centuria published a photo of a member holding a rifle with a Black Sun, the name of American neo-Nazi terrorist David Lane and "15 03 2019" written on it—the date of the Christchurch terror attacks—in a manner reminiscent of the terrorist's own rifles used to carry out the attack.[17]

Centuria, though its roots are of course deeper, is a group still in its infancy, not to mention one born amidst the tumult of a global pandemic. Whether Centuria drifts to become less central to the Azov movement and more peripheral, like some of the initiatives discussed below, remains to be seen.

Official affiliates

Delineating between 'official' and 'unofficial' affiliates and subgroups of the Azov movement isn't a straightforward task. This is particularly the case because, as I show below, many 'official' initiatives themselves blur the lines by having clear relationships and links with 'unofficial' initiatives, and vice versa. Nonetheless, criteria that can be used to try and make this distinction should focus on whether the affiliate carries the branding of the Azov movement, particularly of the National Corps, or whether it is explicitly patronized and promoted by senior leaders of the movement.

One National Corps-branded affiliate is Youth Corps, a series of youth camps across Ukraine that have been held since 2015. Each 12-day camp session (Myachina, 2020) hosts approximately 90 children and youth, and involves many different activities that wouldn't be out of place at any other summer camp, like kayaking and obstacle courses. But Youth Corps camps also teach youth how to assemble and disassemble firearms; each day at the camp is begun with a group recitation of the Prayer of the Ukrainian

17 An archived version of the post and photo can be found at https://archive.ph/JjQC7 and https://archive.ph/GkloF.

Nationalist, an OUN-era paean to Ukraine with lines like "…let me find death in those deeds, a sweet death in agony for you." Youth Corps has received Ukrainian state funding for "national-patriotic education" to host some of these camps (Kuzmenko and Colborne, 2019).

Other affiliates related directly to National Corps include Sports Corps, which hosts mixed martial arts (MMA) training and other sports activities for youth, and Volunteer Corps, a short-lived 2020 effort to provide aid during the initial stages of the COVID-19 pandemic. Despite these Volunteers, their yellow armbands and their branded Volunteer Corps vans being heavily promoted by National Corps from March 2020, by August 2020 the initiative had largely disappeared.

In her capacity as head of the initiative at the National Corps central headquarters in Kyiv, Olena Semenyaka heads the Intermarium project. An early 20th century idea resurrected by the far right of an eastern European confederation of countries to counter both Russian influence and western influence, the project sees countries spanning from the Baltic to the Black Sea and the Adriatic as a bloc of nations that, as Semenyaka has described, can act like a springboard for the revival of Europe; as per a slogan used at its international conferences since 2016, "the heart of Europe beats in the East." Under Semenyaka's direction, the project has hosted a number of international conferences with representatives of far-right movements, along with more mainstream right-wing figures in its most recent iteration in December 2020. I discuss the triumphs and troubles of the Intermarium initiative in more detail in Chapter 6.

Azov Regiment veteran and March of Defenders chief organizer Dmytro Shatrovskyi heads arguably one of the most important Azov affiliates: the Veterans Brotherhood. There are several hundred thousand veterans of the war across Ukraine, of whom only a small minority hold far-right views, have any connection to the far right or are willing to join a far-right movement. In spite of this, groups like Veterans Brotherhood have become "the most influential political actors in veteran organizing"(Friedrich and Lütkefend, 2021). Veterans Brotherhood has played a central role in the launch of Ukraine's veterans' ministry, building relationships with key government officials and positioning themselves as the main defenders of veterans' interests (Bellingcat Anti-Equality Monitoring, 2019). Veterans are, understandably, held in high regard in Ukraine; surveys over several years have suggested those who have fought in the still-hot war are among the most trusted people in Ukrainian society. Veterans Brotherhood and the broader umbrella movement it dominates, the Veterans Movement of Ukraine, takes full advantage of this. These efforts are a means for the far right to insulate their activities from criticism, working alongside non-far-right actors to slowly push itself more into the mainstream of Ukrainian politics and society (Bellingcat Anti-Equality Monitoring, 2019).

Publishing houses also form part of the list of Azov affiliates. Landmark (*Oriientyr*), cofounded in 2016 by Azov ideologist Mykola Kravchenko, publishes works by 20th century Ukrainian nationalists as well as books about Azov's National Militia, the unit's liberation of Mariupol in 2014 and memoirs of Azov fighters.

But Plomin, as discussed in Chapter 2, is the more prominent of the two. Both a book club and publishing house, Plomin's focus has largely been on the metapolitical, hosting lectures and publishing seemingly less overt content like scholar of Indo-European studies Georges Dumesnil, as well as articles about and translations of European far-right thinkers from the Conservative Revolution, Nouvelle Droite and others. Plomin's work has been patronized by Azov leaders; in addition to events in previous years, in April 2020 Biletsky took part of a Plomin online presentation of a book by a Ukrainian nationalist historian.

But much of what Plomin does is considerably less subtle and much more openly extreme. Under the leadership of Azov Regiment veteran Yevhen Vriadnyk—an anti-Semitic promoter of violence (Colborne, 2020)— Plomin has published translations of works by fanatical Romanian fascist Corneliu Codreanu and his Iron Guard as well as Italian far-right terrorists Franco Freda and Pierluigi Concutelli. In November 2020 on its website Plomin published a translation of an article by Theodore Kaczynski—better known as the Unabomber, the U.S. domestic terrorist whose bombing campaign killed 3 people and injured 23 more. The article was referred to positively in the translator's introduction, and includes a photo of a Ukrainian translation of the Unabomber's manifesto, noting that it was published in Ukrainian for the first time in 2019.

A group who managed to garner some media interest before almost disappearing entirely was Silver Roses (*Sriblo Troiandy*). In 2019 and early 2020, Silver Roses was the only female-oriented group in the male-dominated Azov movement, getting noticed for dressing all in black, each woman in the group carrying a rose, at various events and for carrying a coffin in 2020's International Women's Day march in Kyiv with the word 'feminism' written on it (Kovalenko, 2020). Esoteric and eccentric, with its base in Azov's Cossack House, it called itself an "anti-feminist movement," and counted Olena Semenyaka among its members, who participated in public events with them and promoted the group. However, by late 2020 the group had apparently broken with the Azov movement; rumours on Ukrainian far-right Telegram channels suggested it was essentially kicked out of the movement. Silver Roses still appears to exist, though seldom posts content on social media and appears to have no links whatsoever with the Azov movement, describing itself now on Facebook simply as a "women's movement."

Physical spaces are critical for the far right in any part of the world, places where their members can network, form new friendships and generally make themselves at home. For Azov, this includes the ATEK facility in Kyiv as well as the First Nationalist Hub in Biletsky's hometown of Kharkiv, unveiled by the Azov leader in August 2018. This hub has places for meetings, lectures, exhibitions and classes, as well as a gym well-equipped for combat sports training. The Reconquista Club was a Kyiv sports bar owned by Sergei Korotkikh (Roshchina, 2019) that played host to international National Corps conferences in 2018. The bar near the capital's central train station boasted a mixed-martial arts ring that would regularly host fights every Friday night under the direction of Russian neo-Nazi Denis Kapustin (or Nikitin, the surname he publicly uses), as

I myself witnessed in person (Colborne, 2019b). However, it has since closed.

The most well-known Azov hub has been Cossack House, a formerly disused three-story hotel just off Maidan in central Kyiv. Used by the Azov movement since 2014, when it was used as a mobilization and training centre for what would become Azov, the building is owned by the nearby Cossack Hotel (*Hotel Kozatskyi*), itself a state enterprise owned by Ukraine's defence ministry. After winning a competition to use the premises, Azov renovated it and in 2016 opened a far-right social centre that housed a gym, classrooms, the Plomin literature club and bookshop and even an art studio and tattoo parlour (Boichenko, 2017). By 2021, however, times had become tough for Cossack House; the building reportedly no longer has electricity, heating or water, and Azov figures claim a shady investor is trying to force them from the property.

These official physical spaces provide a home for much more extreme figures within the movement. Russian neo-Nazi Alexey Levkin and his National Socialist Black Metal (NSBM) record label and shop, were able to make their home at Cossack House. At one point one could also take yoga classes there from Kirill Radonskiy, a Moscow-born esoteric neo-Nazi with a tattoo of Savitri Devi who read a poem praising Hitler at Wotanjugend's 2019 Fuhrernacht. The same situation exists at Kharkiv's First Nationalist Hub, from where members of openly neo-Nazi groups discussed below, like Wotanjugend and Nordstorm, regularly share photos of themselves in action at what is clearly identifiable as the Hub's gym.

Unofficial affiliates

Groups or initiatives that can be described as 'unofficial' affiliates, like the ones below, differ from more official ones in that they lack clear Azov-related branding (e.g., not using the same logos) and that they are seldom if ever promoted publicly by senior leaders of the Azov movement. Moreover, these unofficial affiliates are usually smaller than official ones—sometimes the initiatives of one or two Azov movement members—and tend to be more much extreme in their views and their actions.

Wotanjugend, under the leadership of Kyiv-based Russian neo-Nazi Alexei Levkin, is probably the most infamous of these. Wotanjugend's stated goal is to be a "mini-university for supporters of right-wing ideology," a "hardcore" group too extreme for the mainstream (Colborne and Kuzmenko, 2019). The neo-Nazi initiative made its home in Ukraine in 2015, when Levkin and other Russians came to fight with the Azov Regiment. As I discussed previously, under Levkin's leadership Wotanjugend has promoted the manifestos and writings of far-right terrorists and even organized 'Fuhrernacht,' a night of literal Hitler worship. Levkin, who was arrested for double murder in 2006—the charges were later dropped— also organizes the neo-Nazi black metal Asgardsrei festival, an international gathering last held in December 2019. Levkin has links to Centuria, being readily identifiable from photos as a participant in the organization's events, and also gave several online lectures in early 2020 to Centuria's predecessor National Militia.

A related group, based in Kharkiv, is NordStorm. One of its apparent leaders, identifiable in photographs from his tattoos and towering frame, is Kharkiv resident Oleh Fadeenko, who has been active in National Corps and National Militia and was one of the leaders of the Centuria column at the 2020 March of Defenders of Ukraine. NordStorm is openly neo-Nazi, with its Telegram channel full of open praise and quotes of Adolf Hitler and, not surprisingly, explicit anti-Semitism and calls for violence. NordStorm focuses on combat training, and its members seem to enjoy knives; the group hosted a knife fight tournament on Hitler's birthday, a tournament which Centuria promoted on its Telegram channel. NordStorm also hosted a July 2021 knife fight tournament in honour of Sviatoslav the Brave's conquest of the Khazars, a tournament in which Centuria members also took part.

A more recent addition to this scene is Avangard which, while originally formed in 2017, became particularly active in 2020. The group is led by Yevhen Vriadnyk and Serhiy Zaikovskyi of Plomin, who I spoke to alongside Semenyaka in December 2018. Zaikovskyi, like Vriadnyk, is openly anti-Semitic; in a not-so-metapolitical move, Zaikovskyi publicly posted photos of himself giving Hitler salutes and using Nazi slogans at the Asgardsrei festival in 2018 (Colborne, 2020). The small group of at best a few dozen is based in Kyiv and in Mykolaiv, Vriadnyk's hometown. Aside from its militant social media rhetoric, Avangard focuses on combat and tactical training; several members of the group, including Zaikovskyi, claimed in 2021 to have received military training and served on the frontlines of the war in eastern Ukraine with Freikorps, a Kharkiv-based far-right group I discuss in more detail below.

In 2021, several more of these small yet extreme initiatives emerged. Among these were Alternativa, little more than a gang that has among other things filmed itself assaulting people who were consuming alcohol in public. One of the group's leaders is Mikhail Shalankevich, a Russian who was a member of a group centred around infamous neo-Nazi Maksim Martsinkevich, or Tesak. After being convicted for assault and theft, Shalankevich came to Ukraine in 2019 or 2020, and is identifiable in numerous official National Corps photos as a party activist; he was convicted of assaulting a Ukrainian journalist in September 2021, though received only a suspended sentence. Another National Corps activist in Kyiv, Iryna Letyen, started up a neo-Nazi group called Solaris which focused on anti-LGBT actions, including an attack on a screening of an LGBT documentary film in May 2021. Like their leaders, many if not all members of these groups appear to be members of other groups as well, particularly National Corps. This makes these sorts of small initiatives almost like their own 'brands,' perfect to wear while taking part in, for example, anti-LGBT violence that National Corps tends not to publicly engage in.

Also included among these unaffiliated groups are organizations across Ukraine who provide combat and tactical training to interested participants for a fee and, like the groups discussed above, have some relationship to the Azov movement. Civil Safety, an organization cofounded by Azov veteran Daniel Kovalchuk, provides tactical training, including firearms training at its own shooting range in Kyiv. Civil Safety has provided training sessions at Azov's Cossack House as well as to Azov's National Militia.

Another group, called School of Courage, is based in Hlukhiv, a small city in northern Ukraine just a few kilometres from the

Russian border. In one March 2020 multi-day training session of dozens of people that included extensive tactical training, School of Courage reportedly also trained a 19-year-old German who said he came from Berlin for the training (Nedelia, 2020). In a 2019 workshop with first-year college students, School of Courage's leader reportedly taught students specifically about the Azov Regiment (Sumy National Agrarian University, 2019); in December 2020 School of Courage members took part in a knife fight tournament in Kharkiv with, among others, members of Centuria and Nord-Storm.

Vinnytsia's Molot Group, who incorporates the neo-Nazi Black Sun into its logo, advertises and promotes its tactical training on its Instagram page. Molot Group appears to have a relationship with the above-mentioned Avangard, and shared a photo of a 2017 training session—its "first joint rotation to the east," it claimed—with members holding a Wotanjugend flag. One individual associated with Molot Group—tagged in Instagram photos by Molot Group's self-described team leader—appears to be a serving soldier in Ukraine's armed forces, even posting a certificate claiming he had taken part in a UK-led training mission (Operation ORBITAL) in August 2020. A month before, this individual also posted a photo of a banner with a barely-pixelated swastika. Loosely translated from Ukrainian, the banner read (my asterisks) "a truce will come when all you f**gots f*cking die"[18] along with his caption (in Russian) reading "it's a good day to kill someone."[19]

Independent organizations

There are several far-right groups in Ukraine have function or present themselves as independent organizations, but have clear relationships and links to the Azov movement.

Tradition and Order is an avowedly Christian far-right group that paints itself as a defender of 'conservative' values. Despite its

---

18 "Перемир'я настане коли ви підари всі здохнете нахуй!" ("*Peremyr'ia nastane koly vy pidari vsi zdokhnete nakhuy!*").

19 "Отличный день что-бы кого-нибудь убить" ("*Otlichnyy den' chto-by kogo-nibud' ubit'*").

heavy self-promotion on social media, Tradition and Order is estimated to be relatively small, perhaps fewer than 100 members. Led by Bohdan Khodakovsky, Tradition and Order has its roots in the neo-fascist group Revanche; Khodakovsky and some of his Revanche colleagues were detained by law enforcement and found to be in possession of weapons, including grenades. Tradition and Order emerged in 2016, and began working with forces aligned with then-president Petro Poroshenko (Krakowsky, 2016). After the 2019 elections, Tradition and Order began cooperating more closely with the Azov movement, and has been strongly alleged to be under the patronage of Azov figure Sergei Korotkikh (Dumskaya, 2020); the group is also close to Kyiv-based Russian neo-Nazi Denis Kapustin. Tradition and Order focuses its energies on anti-LGBT actions, including intimidating and attacking LGBT events and premises of LGBT organizations in Ukraine—attacks that are seldom properly investigated by authorities.

With a name based on the right-wing nationalist paramilitaries in interwar Germany that helped pave the way for the Nazis, Freikorps isn't interested in subtlety. Founded in 2017, Freikorps is made up of people wanting to gain combat experience (Friedrich and Lütkefend, 2021) and has at most a few dozen core members. A Kharkiv-based organization, co-founder Georgiy Tarasenko has been involved in the National Corps. On the streets, Freikorps attacks its perceived political enemies, particularly LGBT activists, and did so particularly at Kharkiv's first-ever Pride event in 2019 (Sukhrakov, 2019). While in April 2020 Ukraine's justice ministry sued to try and get the group disbanded, later that same year Ukraine's veterans' ministry officially recognized as a volunteer unit. Freikorps, as noted above, provided combat training and even an apparent opportunity for combat experience to members of Avangard in 2021.

Based in Uzhhorod, a city in far western Ukraine on the border with Slovakia, Karpatska Sich is a neo-Nazi group that has, among other things, promoted the Christchurch terrorist's manifesto. The group is led by Taras Dciak, a co-founder of Azov Civil Corps' chapter in the region in 2015; the group has cooperated with the Azov movement on protests, actions and even international conferences. The group is also allegedly involved in criminal activities, including smuggling (Gorbach, 2018).

Beyond Azov

The Azov movement, particularly after 2019, has consolidated its already-dominant position on Ukraine's far-right. While there are several smaller far-right groups and relatively prominent individuals outside of Azov's orbit, today few if any of them appear to have any interest in trying to challenge Azov's dominance or to clash with the movement in any significant way. The only group to have done so is the Honor group, led by former National Corps Kyiv leader Serhii Filimonov and former deputy chair Nazariy Kravchenko, a conflict which I discuss in the following chapter.

Right Sector, in the immediate wake of the revolution in 2014, looked to be the movement that would carry the mantle for the country's far-right forces. However, Right Sector didn't take long to underwhelm, with its leader Dmytro Yarosh winning a measly 0.7 percent of the vote in an ill-fated run for the presidency in May 2014. Unlike what would become Azov, Right Sector chose a path of confrontation rather than cooperation with Kyiv's post-Maidan authorities—a confrontation they lost. By 2015 Right Sector had already become a collapsing, fragmented movement; today Right Sector and its few hundred members cooperate often with the Azov movement, including as part of the same electoral coalition in 2019. Right Sector still has a small affiliated military unit, Ukrainian Volunteer Corps, one of the few remaining independent military units whose presence on the frontlines is tolerated by Ukraine's government. Still, Right Sector has nowhere near the presence or influence it had in early 2014.

Even groups that have conflicted in the past with Azov now cooperate on occasion, particularly C14, now technically called Foundation for the Future after a rebranding in 2019-20. C14, as it is still most commonly known, is led by Yevhen Karas, a man with more than a decade of experience as a provocateur on Ukraine's far right. Karas has a long history of violence, even operating a "torture chamber" (Risch, 2021) during the revolution in 2013-14 where he and his C14 colleagues assaulted police officers and those they claimed to be pro-Yanukovych thugs. C14 is assumed to have several hundred members, mostly in Kyiv.

Karas has long been dogged by allegations about his and his group's relationships with powerful political forces, particularly to the SBU (Security Service of Ukraine, *Sluzhba Bezpeky Ukrayiny),* with whom Karas has admitted cooperating (Kondratova, 2017). In a strange 2013 episode, Karas and a number of C14 comrades even made a trip to Moscow, where they attacked the office of the *Komsomolskaya Pravda* newspaper whose editor, they claimed based on scurrilous reports, was involved in the exploitation of Ukrainian women. Afterwards, *Komsomolskaya Pravda*'s editor alleged Karas and company were simply "hired" by United Russia—Vladimir Putin's party—to attack the newspaper because of a controversial article the paper had published months before that had upset several high-ranking United Russia members (Luchistaya, 2013).

Karas has clashed with Azov figures in the past—particularly Sergei Korotkikh in the lead-up to the 2019 presidential elections—but since then the relationship between Karas and the Azov movement has warmed to the point where they have cooperated in several protests and actions.

One fringe figure who has tried to make a name for himself outside Azov is Oleksiy Svynarenko, a Kyiv resident and former Right Sector member who runs a Telegram channel devoted to doxxing left-wing and liberal activists. Svynarenko, who is alleged to be close to Azov's Sergei Korotkikh (Coynash, 2021), has been involved in multiple acts of political violence, at one point even claiming in now-deleted social media posts to have killed Berkut officers on Maidan in 2014. In a lengthy 2020 Telegram post, Svynarenko discussed in detail about how and when those on the far right should assault or even kill their perceived enemies. In a July 2021 post, Svynarenko further admitted that "grey funding schemes," among other things, "have contributed to the development of right-wing movements [in Ukraine.]"

It is this world of so-called "grey funding schemes"—part of the opaque, cloudy world of powerful connections and alleged criminal behaviour that envelops Ukraine's far right and, of course, the Azov movement—that I turn to next.

Chapter 4: In the Shadows

In May 2020, Nazariy Kravchenko claimed that he and Serhii Filimonov, former head of the Kyiv branch of National Corps, had been invited for a "conversation" with Andriy Biletsky at the Azov movement's ATEK facility in Kyiv's western outskirts.

It was apparently anything but a normal conversation. "They collectively tried to persuade us not to support Serhii Sternenko," Kravchenko said. "Their main arguments were blows to the head and interrogations."[20]

Kravchenko and his colleagues in Honor—a small group centred around himself, Filimonov and Azov veteran Ihor Potashenkov, all of whom left the Azov movement in 2019—had vocally supported a former Right Sector leader in the city of Odesa who had become a popular mainstream activist in Ukraine, charged with a murder he insisted was self-defence.

Filimonov explained more in a Facebook video two days after the meeting. There were some thirty Azov members and security members, all armed, he claimed—Filimonov and his two comrades were reportedly forced to hand over their weapons.

"The door opens, I get hit in the head with an elbow and just about pass out," he alleged (NovyNarnia, 2020). Filimonov further claimed there were threats of "breaking arms" and that Biletsky himself personally assaulted Potashenkov. The crux of the confrontation, Filimonov alleged, was Biletsky wanting to know who was behind the campaign to support Sternenko, seemingly frustrated by the Odesite's mainstream popularity.

Biletsky denied the allegations, but acknowledged there was a physical confrontation. "You don't come to meet friends armed," he said, in reference to the visitors coming with weapons. "I don't consider kicking to be using physical force" (Feshchenko et al, 2020).

While this was a juicy enough a story at the time in Ukrainian media, it was what Kravchenko—who fewer than four years before

20 An archived version of this post can be found at https://archive.ph/z8oH2.

had become first deputy chair of National Corps at its inaugural conference—claimed a few days later that was even juicier.

"I want to confess to the crimes I committed under Biletsky's orders while in NK [National Corps]," Kravchenko wrote on Facebook.[21] Contrary to its public statements that it was funded through membership fees, he claimed National Corps was financed through a shady scheme where members and their families would donate not their own money to the party, but money procured by Sergei Korotkikh, money whose origin Kravchenko claimed not to know. An anti-corruption NGO that monitors political party finances, *Chesno* ("Honest"), subsequently explored and confirmed some of Kravchenko's claims in detail using public financial data.

"This is an organized crime group, not a political party," Kravchenko said (Feshchenko et al, 2020).

I've argued before that the relationship between crime—alleged and actual—and the far right in general is a woefully underexplored one (Colborne, 2021). The same can be said for how the far right is financed (Philip, 2021), where we know too little about how far-right movements fund and sustain their operations.

All of this, of course, applies to Azov. In this chapter I will focus on discussing allegations of shady and outright criminal behaviour—including alleged murders—that have, like a thick cloud of smoke, enveloped Azov from its very beginnings. It's difficult, of course, to prove or state with certainty how and when far-right groups and actors have been involved in criminal behaviour, least of all when there are no charges or convictions for their alleged crimes. This is a particular issue in Ukraine, which is still plagued by corruption, organized crime and weak rule of law, not to mention law enforcement bodies barely reformed from their Soviet predecessors. It also doesn't help that the far right in Ukraine benefits from a degree of patronage and protection from political actors who themselves are dogged with corruption allegations and links to less-than-legal behaviour—a topic to which I turn to first.

21 An archived version of this post can be found at https://archive.vn/FOeFh.

Friends in high places

Arsen Avakov, Ukraine's interior minister from February 2014 until July 2021, is well-acquainted with Andriy Biletsky and Azov's predecessor Patriot of Ukraine. As I discussed briefly in Chapter 1, Avakov first earned his money and influence in the chaos of the 1990s. With several business partners, he slowly built a business empire that include a television network, factories and even an Italian cheese plant (Sukhov, 2018). Former mayor of Kharkiv Hennadiy Kernes—who before his death in 2020 denied claims he started his career as a crime boss (Kupfer, 2017)—accused Avakov of being involved in the death of a business partner as both his regional empire and the allegations of corruption surrounding him grew larger and larger (Sukhov, 2018). Avakov has denied the claims.

Avakov eventually moved into politics, becoming governor of the Kharkiv region in 2005. It was as a powerful regional politician that Avakov first began to patronize Patriot of Ukraine; Biletsky and his colleagues would, aside from assaulting immigrants in the city, attack and raid businesses and markets for the benefit of businessmen and others close to Avakov. But soon after Yanukovych's rise and Biletsky's imprisonment, Avakov camped out in Italy avoiding corruption charges he claimed were bogus. After the revolution in February 2014, Biletsky was released and Avakov returned to Ukraine and became interior minister, where he would once again patronize Biletsky and his Patriot of Ukraine comrades.

It was under Avakov's authority that Biletsky's band of far-right fighters, in May 2014, would officially become part of the interior ministry, and eventually a Regiment a few months later. Azov definitively owes its initial rise to having a friend and backer in one of the most powerful positions in Ukraine, someone who would protect them and allow them to function in exchange for a degree of loyalty. Biletsky even owed his initial foray into politics to Avakov, winning a single-mandate seat in Kyiv in 2014 thanks to the interior minister's support (Likhachev, 2018).

It has been long alleged that Avakov remains a patron of the Azov movement as a whole. Avakov quickly became one of the most powerful people in Ukraine once he became interior minister, even being rumoured to have consolidated his authority in part by collecting potentially damaging information on his political allies and potential adversaries (Skorkin, 2020). Ukraine's interior ministry appears more like a hulking Soviet edifice than many may want to admit – a centralized body with some 300,000 employees responsible for everything from policing to border services, all with a lack of oversight and accountability (Bivings, 2020). Even if one of the motivations for bringing Azov into the interior ministry's fold was to exert some degree of control over them (Gomza and Zajaczkowski, 2019), being a leader of a far-right group with the ear of one of the powerful figures at a country's cabinet table – Biletsky admitted in 2018 he spoke to Avakov several times a year (Buiets et al, 2018) – can only be advantageous.

The exact nature of the relationship between Avakov and Azov has long remained an opaque one. Some observers have suggested that, far from Biletsky and Azov being some sort of puppet or private army acting on Avakov's orders, the relationship is more one of "mutually beneficial cooperation" (Ishchenko, quoted in Deprez, 2019), one where the movement can act with relative autonomy yet still on occasion be tasked to work in the interests of Avakov and his allies. The relationship extends to family: Oleksandr Avakov, the former minister's son, arrested and charged with embezzlement in 2017 but released without bail (Sukhov, 2018), has been known to be close with Azov's Sergei Korotkikh.

Under Avakov's reign there has been a form of "rapprochement" (Likhachev, 2018) between law enforcement and the far right, helping create an environment where the far right has been able to operate with relative impunity. Thanks to Avakov allegedly sabotaging attempts at police reform (Bezruk, 2021), attacks on activists – including but not limited to attacks carried out by the far right – are seldom properly investigated.

It's clear that Azov has been able to exert influence in the powerful interior ministry, with no better example than the figure of Vadim Troyan. A former member of Patriot of Ukraine, Troyan also worked at the time for a key ally of Avakov, where he allegedly led a group of Patriot of Ukraine thugs in a raid of newspaper kiosks in

Kharkiv (Yavir, 2016). In 2014 Troyan became part of the Azov Regiment, rising to be a deputy commander. In November of that year Troyan was appointed, to a chorus of criticism, to head up Kyiv's regional police. In 2017 he became a deputy minister of the entire interior ministry, and in 2019 became deputy chief of Ukraine's national police, a position he still holds as of 2021. Despite heading up a senior position in law enforcement, Troyan was alleged to have had involvement in a bribery case, with his house being searched; afterwards, Ukraine's security services (SBU) denied that Troyan had anything to do with it, something critics saw as authorities protecting him from potential trouble (Sukhov, 2018). Troyan has also been alleged, alongside Sergei Korotkikh, to have demanded a share of a company owned by Svitlana and Roman Zvarych, former allies of Azov who played a role in organizing the Regiment and Azov Civic Corps and who also allegedly helped secure foreign financing in 2014 and 2015 (Yavir, 2016). This demand allegedly came at a time when Troyan was acting head of Ukraine's national police (Burdyga, 2018).

The Security Service of Ukraine (SBU) has long had a chequered history. Formed in 1992 after Ukraine's independence, the SBU is more similar to its Soviet KGB predecessor (Scherban and Halushka, 2021) than comparable agencies in the rest of Europe. The SBU is a "strange hybrid" of a law enforcement and intelligence agency, with broad powers to get involved in cases that have little if anything to do with security (Ponomarenko, 2021). The SBU has long been plagued by corruption, competing factions—including alleged collaboration with the far right—and collusion of its agents in criminal schemes. Its powers are often wielded by state officials, not to enforce the law or to protect national security, but to guard their often corrupt interests in a manner more akin to a protection racket. Western-backed efforts to reform the SBU are in progress as of 2021.

Over at the interior ministry—a competing and similarly-plagued ministry—Avakov resigned in July 2021, a move that surprised many. There has been all manner of speculation as to the reasons why Avakov may have resigned, including the failure to solve the case of Pavel Sheremet, a Belarusian journalist murdered by a car bomb in central Kyiv in July 2016.

It's hard to say whether Avakov's departure will mean there are changes in the cards for Azov. His replacement, Denys Monastyrsky, is a man who has been allied with him in the past. Avakov may well become a 'grey cardinal'-type figure; there is no indication that, despite no longer being in the position, that his influence within the interior ministry and in Ukrainian politics is about to completely fade away (Sergatskova, 2021). Azov, for all the patronage and protection Avakov has allegedly provided over the years, is by no means dependent on the munificence of just one man. Nonetheless, the arrest by Ukraine's SBU of a number of National Corps members in August 2021, alleged to be part of a racketeering and extortion ring, could signal that Azov will not always be as protected.

Azov also seems to have friends in unexpected places. In July 2019, I looked on as National Corps members staged a protest in front of Ukraine's broadcasting authorities in Kyiv demanding that NewsOne, a channel linked to pro-Russian oligarch Viktor Medvedchuk that they said spread "anti-Ukrainian propaganda," have its license revoked. Some six months later, I started to see National Corps promote appearances by its representatives on NewsOne and two other channels linked to Medvedchuk—112 and ZIK—from figures like Sergei Korotkikh, Serhiy Tamarin and then-spokesperson for the National Corps Roman Chernyshev.

These weren't isolated appearances. Based on my own count of announcements on their public Telegram channel, National Corps representatives made 13 appearances on the three Medvedchuk-linked channels from September to December 2019. But from January to April 2020, National Corps representatives appeared 61 times on those same channels, an almost fivefold increase. Afterwards, appearances on these channels decreased and eventually ceased, and in February 2021, when Volodymyr Zelenskyy banned these three channels from Ukraine's airwaves, these same individuals who'd repeatedly gone on these channels cheered the decision to close them.

Why would National Corps' leaders all of a sudden be so keen to accept invites onto a pro-Russian oligarch's channels—one who they'd called a Kremlin propagandist—only to stop those appearances just as suddenly and then cheer those channels' demise? It can't be stated with certainty that there has been any sort of connection, let alone a financial one, between Azov and Medvedchuk; they may have just liked the attention and exposure, particularly ahead of 2020 local elections, and were happy to get it from whoever was willing to provide it. Nonetheless, the experience of watching Azov figure after Azov figure made at least some people in Ukraine question the relationship between the country's preeminent far-right movement and the man that same movement demanded be charged with treason. Azov figures' frequent appearances on these channels even reminded some observers of media tactics used by Yanukovych's party, the Party of Regions, to promote the far right as a "scarecrow" to mobilize the party's voters (Tarasiuk and Umland, 2021).

The same can be said for the eagerness with which the Azov movement opposed a land reform bill in Ukraine. Thanks to a moratorium on the sale of farmland passed by parliament in 2001, Ukraine was one of only a handful of countries in the world where farmers weren't able to buy or sell land—a restriction ironically shared with communist states like North Korea and Cuba. Opening up the land market was a key demand of Ukraine's western partners but was unpopular with most Ukrainians, who feared foreign corporations would scoop up all the land. It was also unpopular with Ukraine's agriculture oligarchs, who dominated the existing land market (Bilous et al, 2020) and thus had a stake in stymying reform.

The land reform bill was also unpopular with Azov, at least officially. In late 2019, National Corps and National Militia led numerous demonstrations against the bill—and used a few anti-Semitic tropes about along the way, complaining that "Rothschilds and Soroses" were waiting to grab Ukrainian land. Azov's efforts culminated in a violent December 2019 protest that left at least 19 people injured, including journalists and police officers hit with rocks and bricks thrown by Azov's protestors (Gaubert, 2019).

The violence left some of National Corps' own apparent supporters confused and disappointed on the party's official Telegram chat.[22] "I wholeheartedly oppose the sale of land," said one, "but today National Militia threw rocks at guys who are just conscripts, contractors for the National Guard," and added they didn't know what side to support. Another chatter, who otherwise spoke positively of National Corps, said "it was just a circus," and "if National Corps hadn't discredited itself with violence and lack of restraint, it would have had more influence in society and more support." Scrolling through the chat on the day of the protest, the land reform issue hardly excited more than a few of them.

The bill was eventually passed in 2020 in a modified form, with no allowance for foreign ownership without a national referendum. However, claims that the protests against the bill were financed by agriculture oligarchs (Povorozniuk, 2020) led, like with Medvedchuk, at least some in Ukraine to ask not only who Azov's allies were, but where Azov was getting funded from in the first place.

Who funds Azov?

There's absolutely nothing untoward about how National Corps, is financed, says its leader. In 2018, in advance of parliamentary elections the following year, Biletsky said that the party was one of the most "transparent" political parties in the country, and that most of their funding came from membership fees. In 2020, the party reportedly took in more than 12 million hryvnia (~€400,000/~$474,000) in revenue.[23]

"We have tens of thousands of activists in the party," Biletsky claimed (Buiets et al, 2018), adding that the minimum membership fee was 50 hryvnia, approximately €1.60, but sometimes activists would pay more. "Due to the fact it's such a huge number of people, we bring in quite a decent amount to the party accounts," Biletsky

22 *"Fludilka Patriotiv"* or, roughly, 'Forum of Patriots'; *"fludilka"* ("little flood") is a slang word used in Ukrainian and Russian for an internet chat room or forum.
23 https://opendatabot.ua/c/40214321.

added (Buiets et al, 2018). "Believe me, we pay much more meticulous attention to this than the huge ruling or monster opposition parties."

But in this same 2018 interview, Biletsky did admit that there were other sources of financing, both direct and in-kind. This included funding from the Militarist chain of military outfitting stores—who produced the National Militia's ubiquitous blue jackets—as well as local businessmen and others who would, in his telling, sometimes donate free real estate or building materials. "If me or the guys in the regions ask [them] for help [...] they'll usually help us with these kinds of things."

But Biletsky's claim that National Corps, to say nothing of the other parts of the Azov movement, is funded by membership fees appears dubious. As I mentioned earlier, the Chesno investigation that looked into National Corps finances in the wake of Nazariy Kravchenko's public accusations suggested that something wasn't quite right. From 2017 to 2019, National Corps officially received more than 8,000 individual contributions from more than 2,000 people and seven companies, for a total of 18.6 million hryvnia (~€580,000; ~$690,000) during that time (Feshchenko et al, 2020). While these donations indeed came from activists all across Ukraine, there's nothing inherently suspicious in these figures, though one might marvel at a marginal far-right party's ability to pull in that much money over just a few years.

But when Chesno looked deeper at the numbers, something didn't make sense. At specific times, there were "rapid and simultaneous" donations from different parts of the country, where the total number of activists donated across the country would rise by some three times (Feshchenko et al, 2020). But what was odder was the fact that, when total contributions to the party went up, the numbers of activists donating stayed largely the same. In short, what was remarkable was "the consistency of the behaviour of hundreds of people, who every two to three months simultaneously intensified their donating and contributed more and more record amounts for the party" (Feshchenko et al, 2020). Chesno noted, among other examples, that there were five separate days on which exactly 20 donors from western Ukraine donated exactly 990 hryvnias, an almost-impossible coincidence. These findings appear to confirm Kravchenko's assertion that the money actually came from the central party headquarters to the regional offices—the source of which Kravchenko claimed not to know—and the regional offices would 'credit' the party with donations in their activists' names. This sort of method of financing, Chesno noted, is something that is supposed to be disclosed to the relevant authorities (Feshchenko et al, 2020).

This analysis, however, couldn't demonstrate the source of the apparent centrally-distributed funds. For his part, Kravchenko claimed that only three people were involved in the scheme: Biletsky, Mykhailo Ivanchuk—a figure in the Azov movement responsible for Biletsky's security—and Sergei Korotkikh, though neither Kravchenko nor anyone else has ever provided any evidence to support this claim.

Biletsky and National Corps denied anything was amiss. "It's 99 percent party members," Biletsky insisted (Feshchenko et al, 2020). "We bring our military experience and our sense of discipline to party activities [...] it's easy for me to inform up to 5,000 people, if need be, to relay that they need to help the party within 24 hours. That's why there's this synchronicity."

There have long been alleged to be particularly questionable or shady sources of the Azov movement's income. Members of far-right groups, as I briefly noted in the previous chapter, have long acted as hired thugs in Ukraine for powerful people willing to pay for their services. Oligarchs, politicians and business leaders allegedly pay the far right to intimidate competitors or opponents in ownership disputes. They try and exploit Ukraine's weak rule of law and take over companies and properties, especially through the help of fraudulent 'rulings' from corrupt judges.

Members of the Azov movement have allegedly long played this role. A number of Azov movement members were arrested in Kharkiv in August 2021, alleged to be part of a criminal group that engaged in racketeering and extortion, particularly in funeral services, that earned up to 1 million hryvnia (€31,000/~$37,000) per month. One of those Azov members arrested, Serhiy Velychko, was also reportedly arrested in Denmark in 2019 for theft along with some of his Kharkiv National Corps colleagues (Poragovorit, 2019). In June 2021, approximately 70 individuals allegedly associated with the Azov movement and Right Sector, clad in balaclavas, barged into Ukraine's largest agricultural market, trying to shut it down at the alleged behest of a rival (Ivanov, 2021). In July 2018, a busload of an estimated 60 armed Azov veterans showed up to a quarry and tried to intimidate employees and owners (GolosUA, 2018). Before it became known as Centuria in 2020, Azov's National Militia also played the role of thugs; in December 2018, approximately a hundred National Militia members attempted to take over a Kyiv shopping centre that was in disputed ownership (Fraza, 2018).

Being thugs for hire can sometimes result in playing on both sides of the fence. In May 2019, activists of National Corps led by Serhii Filimonov – who would leave the movement months later – knocked down fences around a proposed development in a Kyiv park, confronting the developer's representatives on the ostensible behalf of local residents and claiming the construction was illegal. A few weeks later in June 2019, Azov movement members working for a security firm linked to Sergei Korotkikh were visible on site not to oppose, but to actually protect the proposed development against which their Azov allies had fought weeks earlier (Roshchina, 2019). Not long after this, Filimonov and his friends in Honor would leave the Azov movement and come into conflict with their former allies.

Other former senior members of the Azov movement have made serious allegations about its sources of funding. Among them is Oleh Odnorozhenko, a former high-ranking Azov and Patriot of Ukraine member who subsequently fell out with the movement. Odnorozhenko claimed in 2021 that the Regiment was paid hundreds of thousands of dollars per month in 2014 to protect businesses and assets of some of Ukraine's wealthiest oligarchs, even claiming that Azov fighters "constantly complained" they weren't being sent to fight, but to protect oligarchs (Gontar, 2021). Odnorozhenko, however, has not presented evidence to support these claims.

Questionable pasts, questionable presents

In January 2015 Ukrainian troops were taking heavy losses in a battle for the city of Debaltseve and other Ukrainian troops were forced to leave Donetsk airport, the scene of a bloody months-long battle with Russian-backed forces.

At the same time Andriy Biletsky's wife, despite having reported no income for the previous year, bought an apartment in Kyiv for her and her husband that journalists (Glavcom, 2016) estimated to be worth between 2.2 and 4.1 million hryvnia (from ~€70,000/~$81,000 to ~€130,000/~$150,000). This came was as the Azov leader's stated income from the previous year was only 49,000 hryvnia: a paltry €1,500/$1,800 for the whole year. Nonetheless, Azov claimed that the purchase was above board, financed through the sale of previous real estate and the savings of Biletsky's now ex-wife (the two split in 2016).

While it's of course possible that the purchase of this apartment was legitimate, the episode and its timing nonetheless raised further clouds of suspicion around Biletsky. From his openly violent history in Kharkiv in the 2000s to the various allegations discussed above claimed to have taken place under his leadership, it's certainly fair to say Biletsky has long had a questionable past. However, that's something he shares with his senior colleagues in Azov, many of who have what one could charitably call questionable episodes in their own personal histories.

As discussed in the previous chapter, Ihor Mykhailenko was a Patriot of Ukraine member, the Azov Regiment's commander from October 2014 to August 2016, as well as head of the National Militia. He was detained in 2011 alongside Biletsky on charges of attempted murder, and released in 2014. He has also been alleged to have taken part in an armed robbery in 2016 (Furmaniuk, 2016); alongside other Azov veterans, he was allegedly ringleader of a gang robbing banks and armoured vehicles, a group that reportedly was involved in upwards of ten similar robberies (Ukrayinska Pravda, 2016), and involved several individuals linked to Azov. Two of the alleged robbers, including a Latvian neo-Nazi, died after a shootout with police. "I have never been investigated in this case,"

Mykhailenko claimed in 2018 when asked if he was involved (Hlukohavskyi and Hruzdiev, 2018). "The only thing that can be tied to me is that ex-fighters of the Azov Regiment were involved in this case."

Mykhailenko's successor as Regiment commander was Maksym Zhorin, who served in that role from August 2016 until September 2017 and has since become one of the Azov movement's most prominent spokespersons. At a Kyiv college dorm in 2013, Zhorin was reportedly stabbed by a fellow student from Cameroon, who received a suspended prison sentence (Tsybenko, 2013). However, the Cameroonian student claimed that Zhorin assaulted him first and the stabbing was self-defence. "Why should I respect you if you're black?" he claimed Zhorin said to him, alleging Zhorin called him a racial slur before beating him bloody and bruised before he fought back with a knife.

Moscow-born, Kyiv-based Denis Kapustin, who uses the surname Nikitin publicly, has been affiliated with the Azov movement for several years. Kapustin's past as a neo-Nazi hooligan and organizer is well-known, having organized MMA events and provided combat training sessions for a number of European neo-Nazis. His existing networks across Europe – he lived for years in Germany as a young adult and speaks German fluently, in addition to English and his native Russian – have been fruitful for Azov; in the past has helped the movement with its international outreach alongside Olena Semenyaka (Miller, 2018). Kapustin is now primarily active with Tradition and Order and maintains a close relationship with Robert Rundo, the American neo-Nazi who, as of December 2021, lives in Serbia despite having been expelled earlier in the year. German authorities banned Kapustin from Europe's Schengen Area in 2019, since preventing him from travelling to almost all European Union countries.

But Kapustin apparently found himself in even more trouble in Ukraine – trouble he has since somehow managed to escape. A report from German newspaper *Der Spiegel* in February 2019 alleged, based on its sources, that Kapustin had been arrested in October 2018 as part of an drug manufacturing ring. Digging through open sources, including a now-broken link with Kapustin's full name in Ukrainian court documents[24], appear to confirm that this was indeed the case. While the names of those involved are redacted, in one of the court documents someone seems to have forgotten to remove the surname 'Kapustin' in reference to the unnamed suspect's Russian passport. It appears that Kapustin was arrested in October 2018 and charged with being part of a drug manufacturing and trafficking ring, and was specifically noted as being responsible for securing supplies of materials needed to make drugs. However, by 2020 the criminal case against Kapustin—which could have resulted in a sentence of five to ten years if he'd been found guilty—had been dropped for unknown reasons. The ostensibly drug-free Kapustin was found guilty only of possessing a small amount of cannabis for which he received no punishment.

Other Russians with particularly questionable backgrounds have come to Ukraine and made themselves at home with Azov. Among them is Alexey Levkin, the neo-Nazi Azov Regiment veteran and head of Wotanjugend. Back in his native Russia, Levkin was part of a gang of Russian National Unity (RNE) members that allegedly vandalized Jewish and Muslim graves, perpetrated a number of assaults and murdered four people (Tvernews, 2010). Levkin himself was reportedly arrested for double murder in 2006, though charges were eventually dropped.

Another more recent Russian arrival to Ukraine is Mikhail Shalankevich, a member of a gang centred around Maksim Martsinkevich (Tesak), an infamous Russian neo-Nazi who died in prison in September 2020. After being convicted in Russia for assault and theft, Shalankevich came to Ukraine and became active in National Corps—he is identifiable in a number of photos and video from party events over 2020 and 2021. Shalankevich and colleagues would film themselves assaulting people consuming alcohol in

---

24 A now-broken link for Denis Kapustin's full name and patronymic (https://clarity-project.info/person/cb1c0c2b66ebab2d7d18a18a5191be8b) in 2020 led to information about a court case about an unnamed Russian citizen (https://zakononline.com.ua/court-decisions/show/82275459), which in turn, searching in more detail in 2021, led to a now-closed criminal case (Number 761/47791/18), accessible through search at https://reyestr.court.gov.ua/.

public or who they claimed were drug addicts. In July 2021 Shalankevich was caught on film spitting at and punching a Ukrainian journalist, a crime for which he received a suspended sentence.

The Russian with the most questionable background in Azov is undoubtedly Sergei Korotkikh. Born in Russia but raised in Belarus, Korotkikh is known to have attended a KGB college there in the early 1990s, leading many today to accuse him of being an agent of Belarus' KGB and/or Russia's FSB—accusations that weren't helped by an August 2021 leak of a video and signed letter, purportedly from Korotkikh, allegedly admitting in the mid-2000s to collaborating with the FSB. He was active in Belarusian and Russian far-right groups in the 1990s and 2000s, including Russian National Unity (RNE)—who have been accused of working with Russian and Belarusian security services—and, later, the National Socialist Society (NSO), itself accused of being linked to the FSB. Korotkikh would be expelled from NSO in 2007 for a number of apparent misdeeds, including financial improprieties and distributing pornography. Korotkikh was allegedly involved in assaulting Belarusian opposition activists alongside RNE colleagues in 1999, detonating a bomb in Moscow in 2007 and was also detained alongside Martsinkevich in 2013 for stabbing an anti-fascist activist in Minsk (Reporting Radicalism, 2021). Korotkikh reportedly took part in conflicts as a foreign fighter in the late 1990s in the former Yugoslavia and in Chechnya, and then allegedly as a private military contractor in Latin America (Yavir, 2016). In 2014, he came to Ukraine and fought with the Azov Regiment, and controversially received Ukrainian citizenship from then-president Petro Poroshenko in December 2014.

Korotkikh's 2016 income declaration—public because at the time he was an employee of Ukraine's interior ministry, ostensibly in charge of security for strategic facilities—revealed that, despite his official yearly salary of 78,000 hryvnia (~€2,400/~$2,900), he was doing quite well for himself. Korotkikh owned one apartment and part of another, a watch and pen worth more than $10,000 and, of all things, a Czech combat training aircraft. On top of this, Korotkikh declared possession of $223,000 and €135,000—all in cash—

and was apparently in good enough financial shape to lend someone €565,000, as per the declaration.

Korotkikh also owned the Reconquista Club sports bar and combat sports venue where he would watch fights accompanied by bodyguards, fights that were overseen by fellow Russian Denis Kapustin. Korotkikh appears to have become close over late 2020 and 2021 with other Russian exiles in Ukraine as well, including Levkin and Shalankevich. Relatedly, several sources independently suggested to me in 2021 that, according to their knowledge, there has been a conflict brewing within the Azov movement between Andriy Biletsky and Korotkikh, who appears to be building up a separate base within the movement under his patronage.

Since his arrival in Ukraine, Korotkikh has amassed a long list of alleged misdeeds. It has been claimed that Korotkikh took almost $200,000 to help seize the ATEK compound in Sviatoshyn in suburban Kyiv for a company who disputed the land's ownership. When Azov seized the compound in 2014, where the movement remains to this day, Korotkikh and comrades reneged on their word and made it their own, according to the company's lawyer (Burdyga, 2018). Korotkikh has been rumoured to be involved in a number of criminal enterprises; though some of these may well be without foundation, Korotkikh made an apparent admission in a leaked private message in 2014 that he was "running contraband" near Odesa, a known hub of smuggling in Ukraine (Furmaniuk, 2017). Korotkikh has been accused by others on the far right of having thugs on his behalf assault rivals and perceived enemies (Proskuryakov, 2021), including the Azov veterans and former National Corps members in Honor (who themselves are no strangers to violence). Still, Korotkikh and others within the Azov movement have been accused of far worse.

Mysteries and suspicions

Senior figures in the Azov movement, particularly Sergei Korotkikh, have been publicly alleged to have been involved in a number of mysterious deaths, including alleged murders. The death of Vitaliy Shishou, a Belarusian exile activist who co-headed the

"Belarusian House" in Kyiv in August 2021 raised suspicions not just of Belarus KGB involvement but of Korotkikh's, given his questionable past and the fact he was linked with Shishou and particularly to Belarusian House's other leader, Rodion Batulin, a Latvian citizen who was banned from re-entering Ukraine by the SBU in August 2021.

Artem Merkulov, an Azov Regiment veteran, was brutally beaten to death in Mariupol in July 2015. Another Regiment veteran, unnamed in court documents, was convicted of killing him in 2019: he stomped and kicked Merkulov repeatedly in the head as he lay on the ground. The wife of another allegedly murdered Azov veteran discussed below, Larysa Babych, alleged to a Russian media outlet in 2021 that Merkulov was killed because of a dispute with Korotkikh; Merkulov apparently disapproved of one of his alleged criminal schemes (Perevozkina, 2021). Court documents in Merkulov's case—a case which wasn't brought to court for two years—state that there were at least three other Azov Regiment soldiers present when Merkulov was beaten to death. While the case was originally tried as murder, the unnamed Azov Regiment veteran was convicted of a lesser charge of 'intended grievous bodily injury' and sentenced to four years in prison but was reportedly freed on time served (Shak, 2019).

Other former Azov members and Regiment veterans have died in what some have considered suspicious circumstances. A senior Patriot of Ukraine member and Azov Regiment veteran, Vitaliy Kniazheskyi, was arrested alongside Biletsky for attempted murder in 2011. Kniazhesvkyi testified against Biletsky during the investigation; in response, Biletsky assaulted his comrade, though the two apparently patched up their differences (Reporting Radicalism, 2021). In July 2017 Kniazheskyi's body was found in a forest outside of Kharkiv, dead from an apparent self-inflicted rifle wound to the chest. Kniazheskyi's friends and colleagues, however, strongly disputed that he would ever kill himself (Vernyhora, 2017).

Though he has denied it, Sergei Korotkikh continues to be dogged by allegations that was involved in the 2016 murder of Belarusian journalist Pavel Sheremet. While many allege that Sheremet was murdered by Russian or Belarusian security services, two Belarusian journalists have alleged Korotkikh killed Sheremet in revenge for the 2000 conviction of a friend and relative of Korotkikh's for the murder of Sheremet's colleague Dmitry Zavadsky (Burdyga, 2021). Another claim, from a man charged with an attempted assassination of a Chechen soldier in Kyiv, alleges that Sheremet was murdered because he had discovered the apparent role of Korotkikh in the murder of Russian opposition politician Boris Nemtsov (Reporting Radicalism, 2021). Korotkikh has denied that he or anyone from Azov was involved in Sheremet's murder (Miller, 2017). To date, no claim of Korotkikh's alleged involvement in Sheremet's murder has ever been substantiated, and the case remains unsolved.

The case of Yaroslav Babych, oft-discussed in Ukrainian media since his death in 2015, remains the highest-profile death alleged to have involved key Azov figures. Babych had associated with Azov's predecessor Patriot of Ukraine and became a senior figure in the Azov Regiment, at one time heading up its training and mobilization centre. In July 2015, he was found hanged in his home outside of Kyiv in what police officially deemed a suicide.

But Babych's widow, Larysa Babych, has contended since 2015 that her husband was murdered. Yaroslav Babych, Larysa has claimed, had been in a dispute with Biletsky and Korotkikh (Perevozkina, 2021). Her husband was responsible, she claimed, for securing financing for Azov from the Ukrainian diaspora (Hromadske, 2016) and was likely murdered because of a dispute over how funds were to be distributed (Perevozkina, 2021). Larysa Babych has also claimed that she was pressured as part of police investigation to accept their version of events, and further claimed (Chernysh, 2019) that fingerprints were erased from the scene.

Aside from Larysa Babych, former senior Azov member Oleh Odnorozhenko alleged in 2018 that Biletsky personally ordered Yaroslav Babych's murder. Odnorozhenko further claimed that Korotkikh and an associate, Sergei Korovin, carried out the murder. Odnorozhenko alleged that Babych had come into conflict with Biletsky over the direction of the organization, including how it was allegedly funded. Azov denied these allegations, accusing

Odnorozhenko of lying (Kulichenko, 2018). Odnorozhenko reportedly left Ukraine after turning against his former allies, and his brother was reportedly assaulted by unknown attackers (Chernysh, 2019).

Sergei Korotkikh has been alleged to have perpetrated a particularly grisly murder in Russia. In August 2007, a disturbing video appeared on the Russian internet showing two men, bound and kneeling, with a swastika flag behind them (Reporting Radicalism, 2021). Two masked figures calling themselves "national socialists" then brutally murder the men. Israeli film director Vlady Antonevycz alleged in a 2015 documentary about the murders that those behind it were NSO co-founder Dmitriy Rumyantsev, Maksim Martsinkevich (Tesak) and Sergei Korotkikh. "Tesak filmed, Rumyantsev witnessed and Malyuta," said Antonevycz, using one of Korotkikh's nicknames, "cut off the heads" (Fanailova, 2016). Korotkikh's defenders online reject his alleged involvement in the murder, some claiming the video was shown to be a fake despite Russian authorities confirming its authenticity in 2008. In August 2021 Russia's powerful yet notoriously repressive Investigative Committee filed murder charges against Korotkikh for the alleged crime.

As I alluded to at the beginning of this chapter, reporting on unproven allegations, particularly ones yet to be if ever tested in a court of law, is a dicey task. Covering the world of Ukrainian political life, one is exposed to all sorts of rumours, claims and counterclaims about all sorts of figures, including those on the far right. Reporting every single one of those in any context would be irresponsible, to say the least: I've been told a number of allegations related to Azov, and am aware of many more, that I have chosen not to include in this chapter. I've focused in this chapter on those allegations that are, for the most part, already a matter of public record and those that are in Ukrainian and international public interest to discuss.

While clarity may never come for some of the claims that have been made about Azov over the years, one thing is certain: there is no shortage of people in Ukraine feel that Azov is a criminal organization, one that has benefited from the protection of powerful interests—including those Azov has claimed to oppose—and, above all, one that is far from the organization it portrays itself to be.

Chapter 5: Mainstreams and Extremes

Just down the street from Ukraine's parliament, Eduard Yurchenko and a half dozen young National Corps activists held up a banner outside the doors of a government office building. A longtime far-right figure who among other things records videoblogs for National Corps' website, Yurchenko and his comrades were there in June 2020 to protest proposed amendments to a language law.

At first glance, little if anything about this looked like it could be the work of a party that had been dubbed a "nationalist hate group" by the U.S. State Department in 2019. Their professionally printed blue-and-yellow banner had a slogan emblazoned on it that might have seemed uncontroversial to most passers-by: "We have to secure the existence of our country and the future of Ukrainian children."[25]

But for the far right, those words and that specific phrasing evokes something else. The hate-inspiring "14 words" slogan was crafted by American neo-Nazi terrorist David Lane and remains a favourite of white supremacists the world over: "We must secure the existence of our people and a future for White children"[26]—words barely different at all to what was printed on National Corps' banner. It seemed fitting then that standing next to Yurchenko, in the middle behind the banner helping hold it up, was a Holocaust-denying National Corps activist in her early 20s, one who's publicly posted photos honouring Hitler and, barely a month before in National Corps' official Telegram chat, had declared that "Jews are the enemies of all living things."[27]

---

25 *"My maiemo zabezpechyty isnuvannia nashoi krayini i maybutnie ukrayinsykh ditei."*

26 In Ukrainian, the slogan is usually translated as *"My musymo zabezpechyty isnuvannya nashoho narodu i maybutnie dlia bilykh ditei."*

27 On May 6, 2020, an account known to be that of the founder of the small Solaris group mentioned briefly in Chapter 3 wrote in Russian *"Yevrei – vragi vsego zhivogo,"* denied the existence of the Holocaust and also stated that "this is just a fact" (*"Eto prosto fakt"*). An archived version of her 2020 Telegram post honouring the birth of Adolf Hitler is available at https://archive.vn/acbWY.

The Azov movement puts on a deliberately scripted show. On the front stage there's a moderate performance, crafted for the way they want the public to see them. But what's behind the scenes on the back stage is unsubtle, extreme and something Azov would prefer to keep out of the spotlight. In this chapter I discuss how Azov makes ample use of doublespeak—deliberately sanitized and deceptive rhetoric to mask extreme ideas—as well as public relations, branding and communication strategies to try and push itself into the mainstream with sometimes worryingly little resistance.

Doublespeak

Every organized political movement, including those on the far right, crafts a specific message for its intended audience. But the way the far right chooses its words, packages its rhetoric and frames its discussions of political issues distinguishes it from more mainstream, liberal democratic political forces on both the left and right.

The word 'doublespeak' is loosely drawn from George Orwell's classic novel *1984*, though the word isn't itself used in the text. It's a term that evokes the use deliberately distorted language intended to hide some level of truth, saying something we don't mean to hide what we really mean. If the term draws on anything more directly from Orwell it's the concept of 'doublethink', which he described in the novel as "the power of holding two contradictory beliefs in one's mind simultaneously, and accepting both of them" (Orwell, 1949).

Doublespeak is not just something the global far right has practiced for decades, but something fundamental to how it communicates at the core. After the horrors of Nazism the far right realized, unsurprisingly, that its credibility had been destroyed and that they could only overcome this by harnessing the power of euphemism (Griffin, 2014). This mentality underpinned far-right ideological currents like the Nouvelle Droite, whose theorists understood how they needed to communicate if they wanted their ideas to have any impact. Far-right movements the world over have generally jettisoned blatant racism, anti-Semitism and overt fascist and

Nazi symbolism in the way they communicate and present themselves to the public. Decades later these movements have deliberately borrowed and aped the language of liberal democracy, "making invisible…radical, counter-democratic aims via the euphemized language of reform" (Feldman and Jackson, 2014). They're contradictory to the core—mainstream, but also simultaneously extreme.

Those contradictions are no accident. One way to think about this is in terms of a 'front stage' versus a 'back stage' (cf. Mudde, 2000). The front stage is for public consumption, including for voters, media and key elites and opinion formers. This is where you see the scripted performance, the way a far-right movement wants you to see it. There's often little to nothing about it that would strike you as particularly extreme, something you might be even more inclined to believe when the spokesperson offstage keeps telling you that this is the case.

But things will look very different if you sneak a peek backstage. Unlike the scripted scene you just saw up front, the back stage is where those who make up the movement, including senior members and even leaders themselves, are doing what they don't want you to see—praising violent neo-Nazi terrorists, throwing up Hitler salutes, preparing to assault their perceived enemies and generally acting and speaking much more like fascists and Nazis of the 1930s and 1940s than they'd like to admit. But the backstage needs the front stage, and vice versa. To borrow Roger Eatwell's phrasing about fascism (1992), far-right movements have both an "esoteric" and "exoteric" appeal: "[the] former refers to the ideological nature of discussion among converts, or in closed circles. The latter refers more to what is considered wise to say in public."

It should be obvious by this point that Azov is well-versed in doublespeak, experienced in putting on a front stage show while trying to keep the spotlights from shining backstage. This is particularly the case if we look at how the Azov movement approaches anti-Semitism.

In the wake of the 2014 revolution, there has been a heated debate about the degree to which anti-Semitism is a problem in Ukraine. Some Ukrainians have argued that there has been a rise in anti-Semitic sentiments and incidents (cf. Colborne, 2019e), a theme often amplified by Russian state media. But other Ukrainians, particularly those generally more pro-western in orientation, insist that anti-Semitism in Ukraine is no more significant than in many other countries, and point to the fact that Volodymyr Zelenskyy, elected president by a landslide victory in 2019, is Jewish. The reality, I would argue from experience covering and writing about the issue in the country, lay somewhere in between. Anti-Semitism in Ukraine may not be as bad as portrayed by some, particularly in Russian state media sources. But anti-Semitic sentiments still very much exist in Ukraine, particularly on the far right, and occasionally pop up in mainstream political discourse.

Officially the Azov movement, and especially National Corps, has no time for anti-Semitism. National Corps' Olena Semenyaka, the main international spokesperson for the entire movement, personally told me in 2018 that Azov "doesn't have any issue with Jews or other ethnic minorities." Sitting alongside Semenyaka, Plomin's Serhiy Zaikovskyi tried to reinforce that, telling me the Azov movement even had Jewish members.

This isn't a bubble that takes long to burst. Barely a week later, Zaikovskyi was posting Instagram photos of himself Hitler-saluting and chanting "Sieg Heil" at a neo-Nazi concert, and continues to post openly anti-Semitic content on Telegram (Colborne, 2020). Semenyaka, despite pleading that Azov has no issue with Jews, would later give an interview to a neo-Nazi organization stating that "having had a minority of Jews involved within our nationalist political sphere has damaged our reputation" and that Jews with "ties to the (sic) international capital" would be expelled from Ukraine if Azov ever took power.[28] Andriy Biletsky, for all his contemporary insistence that he has never held anti-Semitic views, worked for IAPM, a notorious anti-Semitic institution and publicly

---

28 These quotes are from an undated interview Semenyaka gave to the neo-Nazi Nordic Resistance Movement (available at https://archive.vn/oHzWP). In a March 2020 post on her Facebook account (she has since been banned from Facebook; the post is archived at https://archive.is/Kc3hr), Semenyaka complained about a "non-authorized deciphered version" of her words to NRM being quoted but did not deny these words were hers.

made anti-Semitic statements in the 2000s, statements that aren't hard to find online.[29] Other initiatives and individuals affiliated with the Azov movement make ample use of unabashed anti-Semitic rhetoric. For example, Kharkiv-based NordStorm, whose members are active National Corps and Centuria members, wrote on Telegram in December 2020 that "the most important task of the Jews is the destruction and degradation of the white race."

Azov has long played a game with the use of symbols that, despite their doublespeak, are clearly linked to Nazi symbolism. Azov's logo is a Wolfsangel, a medieval symbol co-opted in various permutations by the Nazis for use in a number of military units. From the time of its initial use in Azov's predecessor organizations in the 1990s and 2000s to the present, they have claimed it represents the letters of the words "Idea of the Nation" (*Ideia Natsii*) in Ukrainian. "We don't use and have never used Nazi symbols, as many in the west think," Azov's Oleksandr Alfyorov has said (Synovitz, 2020). "We follow Ukrainian traditions and use Ukrainian symbols." This is despite Azov's particular Wolfsangel symbol being almost identical to that used by, for example, the U.S. Aryan Nations and the so-called Italian National Socialist Workers Party (Jamieson, 2019).

Like the swastika, the Black Sun is an appropriated Nazi version of an ancient symbol. In recent years the Black Sun has become infamous for its use by neo-Nazis and far-right terrorists, including the perpetrator of the 2019 Christchurch terror attacks, who printed a Black Sun on the cover of his manifesto. It's a symbol important enough for far-right extremists around the world to tattoo on their bodies or post in their online propaganda.

With its twelve *sig* runes—the S-like symbols that form the 'lightning bolt' in the symbol of the Nazi SS—radiating out from a circle, the specific Black Sun that neo-Nazis use is no ancient symbol. SS head Heinrich Himmler had the design specifically made for

---

29 For example, anti-Semitic statements in Biletsky's name on the website of "Patriot of Ukraine" were archived as far back as April 2008 (https://bit.ly/3fUNRKx).

a medieval castle he hoped would become a cult-like SS headquarters. Nonetheless, Azov's open use of the Black Sun in its imagery, including using on the original regiment emblem, led it in 2014 to name the regimental magazine 'Black Sun' (*Chorne Sontse*). Despite the symbol's undeniable Nazi roots, Azov has denied that there is anything untoward about the symbol: "There's no hint of any hostile ideologies here," one of the magazine's co-founders said in 2015. "This is our Ukrainian symbol, and it has a sacred meaning" (Berezhniuk, 2015). How this apparently ancient Ukrainian symbol happens to be identical to the one uniquely commissioned by the head of the SS in the 1930s, as well as to the one used by neo-Nazi terrorists around the world, isn't something Azov seems in a rush to explain.

Branding and visuals

It could be a banner, a party recruitment booth staffed by teenage activists, the party's website or the vans used in 2020 as part of their short-lived COVID-19 volunteer initiative. If it's an official National Corps effort, you'll always see the same two shades of blue and yellow plastered on it.

These colours are obviously intended to evoke those of the Ukrainian flag. I remember walking in central Kyiv in 2019 and being able to pick out the National Corps recruitment booth a few minutes' walk away, just from the colours alone that peeked through the crowds of pedestrians. There's plenty of blue and yellow in central Kyiv, no doubt. But National Corps' chosen shades manage to stand out, different enough from other uses of blue and yellow like on the national flag to stand out and be recognizable as the party's brand yet also still being unmistakably 'Ukrainian'. They're also, not coincidentally, the colours I've chosen for the cover of this book.

It might seem a bit banal to call this much attention just to the colours National Corps uses. But it underscores just how much attention the party, and indeed the entire movement, pays to branding and visual communication. Almost major protest, rally or action hosted by the party is promoted on Telegram beforehand with a branded, well-designed photo advertisement and often a hashtag or short slogan—like "No Capitulation!" or "Medvedchuk behind bars!"—livestreamed on YouTube and promoted afterwards with professional-quality photos and, on occasion, a short professional-quality video recapping the event.

A close look at some of these visuals shows the level of thought that goes into creating the overall spectacle. Photos are often taken from perspectives that makes the number of attendees appear much larger than in reality. Smoke bombs and flares, in addition to giving off an exciting yet intimidating aura, also help obscure numbers and make those assembled look larger.

When it comes to communication, the visual is often more important than we might realize at first. In August 2021, Maksym Zhorin and other Azov leaders hosted a press conference to protest what they called 'repression' of the Azov movement. National Corps chose to do their press conference at UNIAN, a mainstream news agency in Ukraine incidentally owned by oligarch Ihor Kolomoiskyi. But the words coming out of Zhorin's mouth, the party's official tale of repression being mounted against them because several members were arrested for being part of an alleged criminal network, were arguably secondary. In other words, how he looked when he was talking mattered more than what he was actually saying. UNIAN's branding on the wall behind Zhorin made it clear to the viewer that he was speaking from a mainstream venue—a place mainstream politicians also spoke from, though most unlike him probably didn't wear their polo shirts tugged up over their biceps. It was an image not only of being strong, but being legitimate, being mainstream, being normal: as National Corps has described themselves, "the force that can change the country!"

This extends to the way National Corps usually portrays Biletsky and its exclusively male senior leaders. There will almost never be a smile—stern and serious, almost a glare—with hair always cropped short and arms crossed menacingly. One would struggle to find any photo or video of Biletsky published by Azov that doesn't portray the leader looking anything other than ready to pick a fight or lead his men into battle—a look he quite consciously adopted in August 2021, donning his fatigues to lead a column of Azov protesters to Ukraine's presidency.

The importance of visuals for Azov extends deep into far-right subcultures around the movement, particularly into the realm of fashion and tattoos. Sociologist Cynthia Miller-Idriss (2019) argues that visual culture is a means for youth to engage with and become involved in the far right, and isn't explored enough by scholars and researchers. Visual culture on the far right can give youth a greater sense of belonging and identity, and even act as "a mechanism to radicalize and activate extremist engagement" (Miller-Idriss, 2019).

Ukraine has a well-developed far-right visual subculture, particularly around fashion and tattoos. Far-right fashion brands, whether international like Thor Steinar or domestic like Svastone, are ubiquitous among far-right youth in Ukraine. Tattoos are extremely common among all sorts of youth subcultures across Ukraine—in my experience, more common than in many other European countries—and hardly the sole domain of the far right. But far-right youth in Ukraine, particularly young men, are often covered in specific tattoos. Examples include the Black Sun on the elbow, the Azov Wolfsangel and coopted Norse or pagan imagery like the *vegvísir* (a compass-like symbol with roots in Iceland that also resembles a snowflake) or runic letters. Combined with the focus on physical fitness promoted within Azov, a subculture of muscle-bound, fashionable, heavily-tattooed men has developed in Ukraine around the movement, a hypermasculinity also reflected in the way the movement's leaders are presented.

It's hard to find a better word to describe them—these young men in Azov look pretty cool. "Azov has made far-right nationalism fashionable, and they have been strategic in how they portray themselves," said Ukrainian researcher of the far right Anya Hrytsenko (quoted in Miller, 2018). "[It's] helped them to move from a subculture to the mainstream." Even Azov's own spokespeople acknowledge the power of this subculture: "A distinct subculture has been formed around the Azov movement," Olena Semenyaka said in 2019, "and it is easy to distinguish the "Azovians" from [other far-right] activists."

But there's more to Azov's visuals than just a projection of strength and power on the streets. Whether it's photos from anniversaries of key events, like the liberation of Mariupol, the Regiment's annual honouring of its dead in a torchlit spectacle every September or mentions of a senior member's military experience, the movement's official social media never forgets to show its men in uniform. In August 2021, in the wake of his arrest as part of an alleged criminal enterprise, the Azov movement took pains to point out that Kharkiv leader Serhiy Velychko had served in the Regiment on the front lines years before, plastering photographs of him posing in uniform across their Telegram channels. Paired with the constant mentions of the word 'veteran' and 'volunteer', underscoring that the Regiment's fighters willingly went to war in 2014, it was yet another example of how the Azov movement continues to position itself in Ukrainian public discourse: not as extremists, not as criminals, but solely as 'patriots' who have defended and continue to defend Ukraine from its enemies.

A wartime media climate

He may be the leader of a violent far-right movement and have a long, documented history of violence and hateful rhetoric, but Andriy Biletsky has a platform in Ukraine most of his ideological brethren across Europe and beyond would love to have. Biletsky has his own blog, as do many mainstream politicians and public figures, on *Ukrayinska Pravda* (Ukrainian Truth), one of Ukraine's most respected online media outlets. He is often invited on popular political talk shows on Ukraine's main (oligarch-owned) TV networks, including at least a dozen appearances since 2019 alongside swathes of other guests on *Freedom of Speech with Savik Shuster*, one of the most popular talk shows in the country. While it'd be a stretch to say Biletsky is some sort of omnipresent, super-popular figure in Ukrainian media, there are few if any far-right leaders around the world—particularly ones who lead movements as extreme and, ironically, electorally insignificant—who have the level of mainstream exposure Biletsky does.

There has generally been a right-wing, patriotic turn to political discourse in Ukraine since 2014. Slogans, symbols and language that were formerly the domain of the far right in Ukraine have become part of mainstream discourse in Ukraine (Andriushchenko, 2015) and become a boon to Azov and other far right groups. For example, in March 2021 a festival at a popular disused factory space in Kyiv openly used Black Suns, identical to those used by Azov and international neo-Nazis, and runic letters all over its backdrops and banners with little to no discussion in Ukrainian media. The fact that these symbols, slogans and language have been legitimized in public discourse has helped provide "even the most radical [far-right] groups with a largely benevolent or at least neutral media reception," to the extent that leaders of far-right groups like Biletsky have gone from barely being noticed in media to being called on to publicly comment on a number of issues (Likhachev, 2018).

Azov makes use of a number of strategies to get its message out in Ukrainian media. Attention-grabbing spectacles, like confronting police in August 2021 at Ukraine's presidential administration, are designed to get maximum media attention. As I've noted before, Azov figures like Biletsky, Zhorin, Sergei Korotkikh and others have made reasonably regular appearances on talk shows and newscasts in Ukraine across a variety of networks; Azov, of course, has had no shame in the past about frequently appearing on now-closed television channels linked to pro-Russian oligarch Viktor Medvedchuk. Azov also makes use of non-traditional media outlets like Telegram, a hugely popular source of information in Ukraine; unlike in many other countries, Telegram is used not just by the far right but by Ukrainians across the spectrum. While Azov has its own Telegram channels, including the more than 20,000 subscribers to Andriy Biletsky's channel, the movement has been able to get its message out on mainstream Telegram channels. One of the most popular Telegram channels in Ukraine, the Russian-language *Ukraina 24/7*, has more than 400,000 subscribers and has regularly posted content about the Azov movement over 2020 and 2021. However, it's likely that Azov's mentions on these channels is part of the phenomenon known as *dzhinsa* – literally, 'jeans' –

when paid-for content is presented as news, a well-known phenomenon in Ukrainian media. This is apparent when one looks at the laudatory posts about Azov on this channel: it's almost comically obvious that the posts are part of a public relations effort, likely written by Azov representatives themselves.

One of the main reasons why the far right, including Azov, can receive such neutral or even positive media coverage in Ukraine is because of a deep-seated fear of feeding into what are perceived to be Russian propaganda tropes about the far right. Russian state media, to be clear, has long exaggerated the role of the far right in Ukraine. Evoking Soviet propaganda of old with talk of *banderivtsi* and the like, contemporary Russian state media has often used superficial and misleading coverage to present Ukraine as some sort of place on the verge of literally being taken over by Nazis. The issue, however—and something that has been particularly clear for years—is that there actually is a significant far-right problem in Ukraine and that it isn't simply a figment of an overactive Russian state media imagination to say so. This has led to a media environment where anyone domestic or international who writes critically about the far right in Ukraine can find themselves slandered as a 'Kremlin agent' by at least a few Ukrainians and international defenders online. It doesn't help matters that, in Ukrainian media, most discussion of the far right, particularly the Azov movement, comes from outlets like *Strana.ua* that are perceived to not only have pro-Russian leanings but weak journalistic standards. Those more respected outlets in Ukraine that do report critically on the far right, like Hromadske ("Public") or *Zaborona* ("Banned"), are few and far between, and often find themselves the target of criticism if not outright abuse and threats for their work.

But this fear of feeding Russian propaganda tropes has much deeper roots. The fall of communism across eastern Europe produced a groundswell of resurgent nationalism in countries like Ukraine, where nationalism of almost any stripe had been taboo for decades as the most overt form of resistance to communist rule (Subotic, 2019). While western Europe had lived under what historian Dan Stone calls an "anti-fascist consensus" since the end of World War II—that is, "a consensus that fascism had been defeated and that anything akin to it should not be repeated" (quoted in Hajdari, 2020)—communist governments in eastern Europe imposed what Stone calls "an anti-fascism from above." As the decades of communism wore on, this top-down antifascism became rhetorical and superficial as memories of the fight against the Nazis faded (Stone, 2014). After the fall of communism this led to a backlash, a "strong rejection of anti-fascism as a solely Russian creation" (Hajdari, 2020) and a corresponding embrace of some of the nationalist heroes of old, including Nazi collaborators, as a source of inspiration for these newly-independent countries' processes of nation-building. The consequence of this in Ukraine, especially after 2014, is an environment where the act of speaking out against groups like Azov can be painted as little more than a superficial Soviet and thus pro-Russian carry-over. This certainly isn't helped when perceived pro-Russian figures in Ukraine, like former Right Sector figure Ilya Kiva, dishonestly evoke anti-fascism in their own rhetoric. This further helps associate criticism of the far right with being pro-Russian, something that the country's pro-western mainstream obviously has no time for.

Sometimes the far right can exert enough pressure to shut down media coverage it doesn't like. In 2021, a state-funded television channel that broadcasts in Russian to eastern Ukraine, Dom TV, put out a YouTube video that critically discussed the far right in Ukraine. Figures like popular blogger and former Right Sector member Serhiy Sternenko, as well as Azov senior figure Maksym Zhorin, reacted angrily online and demanded that Dom TV remove the clip; a few days later, Dom TV did just that. The fact that the far right was able to successfully demand a state-funded broadcaster remove critical coverage about them is indicative not only of the influence that the far right really has in Ukraine, but of why there's relatively little critical coverage of the far right in the country.

Multiple Ukrainian journalists I've spoken to over the last several years, including those who have written about Azov and other far-right groups, freely admit that they and their colleagues have been afraid to write about them. Some of this fear, they've told me, is more mild: a fear of pressure from family, friends and peers who don't think the topic merits any attention, and a fear of being labeled as unpatriotic or even pro-Kremlin. Worse, however, is the fear of threats, of real-world consequences from far-right actors themselves, particularly when their shady sides they'd prefer to keep out of the spotlight are exposed. Given unsolved murders of journalists like Pavel Sheremet, not to mention a number of assaults on journalists for which no one has ever been punished, this is certainly a legitimate fear for a journalist in Ukraine to have.

One of the primary ways Azov has managed to exploit Ukraine's wartime media environment is by what seems like an exercise in repeating a word over and over again: veteran. Some of the most admired and trusted people in contemporary Ukraine are, not surprisingly, the several hundred thousand veterans of the war. One poll from the summer of 2021 shows that most trusted institution in Ukraine is the country's armed forces, while some of the most distrusted are courts, parliament and government. A similar August 2020 poll included a specific mention of veterans in its list of questions; almost two-thirds of Ukrainians said they trusted veterans of the war, with only the armed forces themselves being more trusted. This is hardly some uniquely Ukrainian phenomenon; for example, Croatian veterans in the Yugoslav disintegration wars of the 1990s still enjoy a great deal of trust and respect from much of the population as well as a considerable degree of political influence.

Even as it's obvious that most of the movement's members have never served in the armed forces—something that the young faces in the movement's ranks make increasingly clear—Azov presents itself as a movement that has fought the enemy, that has acted as a vanguard against that enemy's aggression and, moreover, continues to do so far away from the front lines today. Whenever the movement becomes the target of criticism, or faces what it feels is pressure from authorities, the veteran status of those involved will be played up and promoted. By insulating themselves with the label of 'veteran', they make it difficult for many in Ukraine to criticize them. And when the Azov Regiment in particular is criticized—for example, when American politicians call for it to be designated a terror organization (Colborne, 2019f)—even those who are not on the far right nor fans of the broader Azov movement will defend them. For many in Ukraine, it doesn't matter what Azov believes, whether they're far-right, neo-Nazis, fascists or otherwise—what matters to them is that they fought against Russian aggression and are on their side (Umland, quoted in Montague, 2020). There's a ton of political capital at stake in being a veteran in Ukraine. Azov knows that and has made a heavy investment in it.

The long march through institutions

No matter that he's been dead for almost 90 years and was, of course, a Marxist: Antonio Gramsci continues to have at least an indirect influence on the contemporary far right. Drawing on the Italian's theories of cultural hegemony, German left-wing activist Rudi Dutschke came up with the phrase 'long march through institutions' during the revolutionary tumults of the late 1960s. Dutschke and subsequent left-wing activists and thinkers like Herbert Marcuse argued that the focus of the radical left needed to be less on bringing about an immediate revolution and more on slowly influencing and coming to dominate key culturally significant institutions, like schools, police, armed forces, media and key government ministries, to lay the groundwork for that eventual revolution.

Decades later it's not the left, but the right, that seem to have become the ones talking about a long march. Whether they know it or not, they all have the Nouvelle Droite to thank for turning Gramscian theories of cultural hegemony upside down, shearing them of any left-wing content and giving the postwar far right a new set of tools to try and make their dreams a reality—in short, for giving them the concept of metapolitics.

Metapolitics, as I discussed in Chapter 2, is based on the idea that, if any far-right revolution were ever to happen and be successful it would need to be rooted in the proper conditions. Without changes in social and cultural consciousness—or, as Azov's Olena Semenyaka rather bluntly put it to me in 2018, after having "overcome this psychological resistance to nationalist, far-right ideas" and counteracted a "demonized image" of the far right—there is no hope of revolutionary change. Metapolitics involves a number of different strategies and tactics (Ravndal, 2021), but importantly involves trying to gain influence and dominance in a number of key institutions, including the education sector, the military as well as civil society (Bar-On, 2007).

Azov has been more than willing to go on this long metaphorical, metapolitical march through institutions in Ukraine. To be fair, it probably didn't take all that much time or effort in 2014 to march into Ukraine's powerful interior ministry with Arsen Avakov holding the proverbial gates open for them. Under Avakov's watch, Azov has been able to build and develop significant patronage networks, including alleged criminal networks (Gorbach, 2018), with little fear of police or the courts. The extent to which Azov has been able to consolidate its presence and strengthen its networks thanks in large part to the cover provided by one of the most powerful ministries in the country is a metapolitical coup Azov's friends abroad could only wish they had. To deliberately overuse the metaphor here, Azov's march through institutions established its earliest and perhaps most significant beachhead at the interior ministry, though one that seems under at least some increased fire since Avakov's 2021 resignation.

Azov has also tried to make inroads into education in Ukraine, particularly under the guise of so-called 'national-patriotic education.' The term has been around in Ukraine since before 2014, and mostly on the far right; Andriy Biletsky was a deputy director for national-patriotic education (NPE) at the anti-Semitic IAPM in the mid-2000s (Likhachev, 2014). Mykola Liakhovych, a far-right activist and veteran of the Azov Regiment, was instrumental in pushing NPE into the state organs of post-2014 Ukraine, particularly the Ministry of Youth and Sports.

The extent to which NPE is acknowledged as a policy priority by Ukrainian state bodies suggests Azov's efforts to influence state education policy may have been at least partly successful. According to Ukraine's Ministry of Youth and Sports, NPE is one of the "main vectors" of the Ministry's work, and one that in 2021 was solidified with a plan, approved by Ukraine's cabinet, to continue to develop and promote NPE in Ukraine (Ministry of Youth and Sports, 2021). Even as current state NPE documents make mention of democracy, tolerance and other things not exactly loved by the far right, the main priority of NPE according to Ukraine's Ministry of Education and Science is to form proper attitudes in young Ukrainians "towards the Ukrainian people, Fatherland (*bat-kivshchyna*), state, [and] nation." (Ministry of Education and Science of Ukraine, n.d.) Groups affiliated with the Azov movement, including Youth Corps, received approximately $30,000 in Ukrainian government funds in 2019 for NPE projects (Kuzmenko and Colborne, 2019); in 2021, Azov's Youth Corps received 360,000 hryvnia (~€11,400/$13,000) in funding.[30]

In terms of influencing education in Ukraine beyond NPE, Azov's efforts look to be less systematic. Over the years Azov movement figures have visited schools and given lessons on a number of topics, including on weapons, but these don't tend to happen consistently. Mykola Kravchenko has co-founded a think tank, the Institute of National Development, with other Azov movement members, but it has minimal public presence and appears to seldom publish research or articles. Kravchenko and his think tank have also been behind efforts to influence Ukrainian-language Wikipedia, hosting a 'Wikipedians' forum in June 2021 and seeing the online encyclopedia as a key avenue of influence.

Despite figures like Semenyaka repeatedly noting the importance of universities in any metapolitical strategy for the far right—for example, stating in 2018 that "the modern right needs to carry out a revolution in universities and the education system, in every possible way emphasizing its involvement in it"[31]—Azov doesn't appear to have made any significant efforts to infiltrate Ukraine's universities. While the movement undoubtedly has a few sympathetic academics, researchers and students—and several senior leaders with graduate degrees who fashion themselves as intellectuals—it's hard to see Azov having ever made any bold moves to seize the so-called "laboratories of thought" (Bar-On, 2013) in the manner of their ideological forebears from the Nouvelle Droite. An

30 Information about 2021 funding available from Ukraine's Ministry of Youth and Sports at https://bit.ly/3o9EDiD.

31 An archived version of this interview is available at https://archive.ph/DZfVe.

exception might be made for Olena Semenyaka's abortive 2021 fellowship at Vienna's Institute for Human Sciences (IWM), the withdrawal of which after public outcry caused National Corps to complain that it stymied their dialogue with their allies in the region.

Ukraine's veterans' ministry, on the other hand, is somewhere where Azov wields huge influence. After the ministry was created November 2018, the Azov movement took credit for its very creation; National Corps claimed that it was thanks to the pressure of its Veterans Brotherhood and leader Dmytro Shatrovskyi that "forced" the government to create the ministry (quoted in Bellingcat Anti-Equality Monitoring, 2019). Since its creation the Azov movement and the broader Veterans' Movement of Ukraine (VMU), an umbrella group that Azov dominates, has been able to push its agenda onto the ministry and have its representatives treated as legitimate political actors. According to one veteran and activist (Bellingcat Anti-Equality Monitoring, 2019), the ministry had been "hijacked" by Azov and its allies, a sentiment that by 2021 could be extended to describe the way Azov dominates discussion related to veterans' issues in Ukraine.

Having a far-right movement monopolize the issue of veterans in a country still at war is problematic for a number of reasons. For one, it helps push a stereotype that all of Ukraine's hundreds of thousands of veterans are affiliated with the far right; the fact that some veterans' organizations are linked to the far right has even led some international donors to be hesitant to give money to veterans' organizations, worried that their funds will go to the far right (Friedrich and Lütkefend, 2021). Moreover, with the social capital that comes with being a veteran, Azov's continued domination of the issue and positioning of its Veterans Brotherhood and the umbrella VMU helps legitimize their movement. As veterans become an even more organized force in a country still at war and plagued by longstanding political, economic and social issues, Azov's dominance in this area could prove fruitful for them. But it could be poisonous for the rest of Ukraine; informal organizations run by far-right veterans that engage in combat, tactical and paramilitary training, have access to weapons and are willing to sell their services (Rekawek, 2021) would be a dangerous wild card for any country.

Azov's influence in Ukraine's armed forces extends beyond the Regiment. The Centuria 'order'—not to be confused with the National Militia descendant of the same name—is an explicitly far-right grouping of serving members in Ukraine's armed forces, including officers; while seemingly independent, the Centuria order has clear links to the Azov movement (Kuzmenko, 2021). According to its manifesto, the order is focused on among other things, "the need to save Europe" and to "protect the identity of European peoples from internal and external threats." In 2019, the Centuria order promoted Azov favourite Mykola Stsiborskyi's *Natiocracy* to cadets and future military officers at the Sahaidachnyi National Ground Forces Academy, one of Ukraine's main military training centres. While the order has stated that its work since its founding in 2018 had since become less public and "more subtle and hidden," they nonetheless publicly stated in April 2021 that its members in the armed forces had taken part in military exercises with French, British, Canadian, American, German and Polish military forces working with Ukraine. Moreover, in response to questions about the Centuria order, Ukraine's armed forces stated that they do not screen recruits for extremist views or ties to extremist organizations (Kuzmenko, 2021).

While further research is no doubt needed, it appears that there is an organized far-right presence in Ukraine's military, including a presence linked with the Azov movement, that is freely able to operate and to access military training from western countries. Without at least some far-right presence it wouldn't have been possible, for example, for one of the Ukrainian Ground Forces four operational regional commands to publicly promote Plomin's translations of far-right European authors, even quoting Dominique Venner's work in a 2020 Facebook post.[32] The United States, France, Germany, Canada and many other countries have begun to reckon with the existence and sometimes rise of far-right

32 An archived version of this post can be found at https://archive.vn/6Lsgf.

extremist elements within their armed forces—Ukraine needs to begin to do the same.

Azov hosts a carefully crafted show to present the image they'd like the world to see. With its backstage kept behind the curtain from the front stage, Azov has tried to push itself from the extremes into the mainstream in Ukraine, with at least some degree of success. But it's a different story abroad. Over the last several years Azov has frequently found itself a topic of discussion in international media, the movement being forced to defend itself from a level of scrutiny they're not used to getting at home. Whether it's allegations about the movement providing training to foreign far-right extremists or revelations from journalists like myself about the extent of their international ambitions, Azov has managed to build up quite the reputation for itself beyond Ukraine's borders.

Chapter 6: International Ambitions

We sat there on a spring evening in 2019, in a nondescript café at the end of one of Zagreb's main tram lines. My guest across from me, wearing a grey sweater with "AZOV" on it—in Cyrillic, something you don't normally see around the Croatian capital given its associations with the Serbian alphabet—recounted his time in Ukraine to me.

This was Denis Šeler, a veteran of not only the war in eastern Ukraine but of the war in Croatia in the 1990s. He'd also been a leader of an infamous Dinamo Zagreb hooligan firm, Bad Blue Boys (BBB), that had connections with far-right Dynamo Kyiv supporters.

Šeler told me how he had wanted to go fight for Ukraine, seeing parallels in his own country's battles with Serbian forces in the Yugoslav disintegration wars almost three decades earlier. Eventually, with a group of other Croatians, he made it to Ukraine and joined what would become the Azov Regiment. He stayed in Ukraine, traveling back and forth from Croatia. When I spoke to him he was still working with Azov.

But this wasn't why I wanted to talk to him. By 2019, the fact that he and other foreigners had gone to fight with the Azov Regiment was already old news. I was interested in hearing about why the Azov movement and its international secretary, Olena Semenyaka, seemed to be growing particularly close to figures on Croatia's far right—and why she and others had talked publicly about hosting one of Azov's main international conferences outside Ukraine for the first time in Croatia later that year.

Šeler, however, had much more to tell me. "Biletsky will come next month to Zagreb to officially visit," Šeler said, telling me that he had arranged for Azov's leader to meet with several far-right Croatian politicians.

"Oh, Biletsky will come here?" I responded, trying to sound as unfazed as possible.

"Yeah, yeah," said Šeler. "It was my idea and Azov supports me."

Biletsky, Šeler told me, would be coming to Croatia very soon to meet some of Azov's far-right friends in Croatia. A few months later, at Azov's Intermarium conference in Zagreb, Šeler claimed there would be around 40 people from Ukraine as well as supporters from Poland, Norway, the Baltic states and other countries.

None of this, however, would come to pass. Biletsky never made it to Croatia—only Semenyaka, Mykola Kravchenko and a few other Azov figures made it to Zagreb for that 'official' visit. After I published an article about Azov's connections in Croatia in July 2019, the Intermarium conference in Zagreb never took place at all, and Azov's once boastful international networking presence soon fell almost completely silent.

With what has seemed like boundless ambition, Azov has made considerable efforts to form relationships with far-right figures and movements across Europe and beyond. But thanks in large part to international scrutiny, these efforts have fallen well short of what they'd hoped for. In this chapter I will explore the nature of Azov's international far-right friendships past, present and future, as well as how the movement's seemingly rocketing international ambitions fell back down to earth.

Azov's first foreign friends

From the moment of its birth in 2014 the Azov Battalion then Regiment started attracting considerable attention from outside Ukraine. But this attention came from more than just foreign journalists curious about the unit's ideological leanings. Far-right fanboys from across Europe and beyond were interested in something few if any of them had ever seen before—a military unit with obvious and open far-right roots fighting in an active war on European soil.

The war attracted foreign far-right extremists from around the world to both sides of the conflict. They were motivated by everything from the thrill of war to geopolitical concerns—whether anti-western or anti-Russian, which for them meant anti-Soviet and anti-communist—from those motivated by far-right ideologies to those even wanting to use Ukraine as a stepping stone to a career as a private military contractor (Rekawek, 2020).

Croatia's Denis Šeler was certainly not the first or last foreigner to come to Ukraine to fight with the Azov Regiment. During the hottest heights of the war in 2014 and into 2015, foreigners with far-right or outright neo-Nazi backgrounds, from countries like the aforementioned Croatia, Sweden, the United States and more, made their way into the Azov Regiment's ranks in Ukraine. While exact numbers are hard to come by, there may have been a total of up to 100 foreign fighters in Azov's ranks. Not all of these fighters would have served at the same time, nor would all of them have even had the chance to take part in the heated battles many of them had seen and heard about in spring and summer 2014. Ironically enough, a plurality of these foreign fighters, perhaps half of them or more, came from the country Azov was fighting against: Russia.

By 2014, much of Russia's far-right scene had started to come under considerable pressure from the Kremlin after a previous period of flirtation if not outright cooperation with Putin's regime. Movements like the Militant Organization of Russian Nationalists, better known by its Russian acronym BORN, had long been alleged to have a cozy relationship with the Kremlin (Coynash, 2015). Members of BORN committed at least ten murders, including the killing of human rights lawyer Stanislav Markelov and journalist Anastasia Baburova in 2009. Maksim Martsinkevich's Restrukt movement had once been on better terms with the Kremlin; the late Martsinkevich appeared on pro-Kremlin television channels as part of his anti-LGBT vigilantism and helped reinforce the Kremlin's propaganda against its liberal opposition (Ragozin, 2017). But it didn't take long for these apparent relationships to go south, as some far-right extremists in Russia started to find themselves arrested and prosecuted by Russian authorities.

Since the collapse of the Soviet Union, Russia and Ukraine's far-right scenes have been tightly intertwined as activists, leaders, musical acts and propaganda would go back and forth across the border. The scenes were tight enough that, for years, Russian far-right extremists seeking to evade prosecution would make their way to Ukraine to hide out; before 2015, Russians were able to enter

Ukraine using just a Russian internal passport (Yudina, 2020). By the time of the revolution in 2014 and the outbreak of war with Russian-backed forces in eastern Ukraine, the loyalties of a significant part of Russia's far-right extremist scene lay not with the Russian-backed side but with their Ukrainian opponents taking up arms against Putin, against a regime that had turned on them.

In 2015, it was estimated that there were 50 Russians in the Azov Regiment (Sukhov, 2015). Russian far-right figures who came to Ukraine to join the Regiment's ranks include Sergei Korotkikh, infamous veteran of the Russian and Belarusian far-right scenes, Wotanjugend's Alexey Levkin and Roman Zheleznov, a violent neo-Nazi who once went to jail for shooting a Moscow anti-fascist activist in the head (Ragozin, 2017). Though Zheleznov has since reportedly left Ukraine, most Russians who came to fight with the Regiment have stayed in the country. These include better-known figures who have been given Ukrainian citizenship by presidential decree, like Korotkikh and fellow Russian Nikita Makeev—who praised the Christchurch terrorist and in 2019 attacked a motorcade carrying former president Petro Poroshenko (Colborne and Kuzmenko, 2019)—as well as others who maintain a much lower public profile (Yudina, 2020).

But it was the presence of foreign fighters from mostly western countries that attracted the most media attention in 2014 and 2015. Foreigners in Azov's ranks included fighters from countries like Italy and France, Scandinavian countries like Norway and Sweden, Baltic states like Latvia and even the United States. It doesn't take much searching online to find coverage of western far-right extremists and neo-Nazis who took the trek to Ukraine to fight with Azov. Sweden's Mikael Skillt told a journalist in 2014 that he believed in fighting for the "survival of white people," stated Jews aren't white and added that he wanted to go fight for Bashar Al-Assad because the Syrian dictator was standing up to "international Zionism" (Newman, 2014). The talkative Skillt was accompanied in the Regiment by several other Swedes including Jonas Nilsson, who now reportedly lives in South Africa (Thamm, 2019). Along with Denis Šeler were an estimated 20 Croatians, including Croatian resident and French-born soldier Gaston Besson, who helped organize international recruitment efforts for Azov in 2014 and himself was a foreign fighter for Croatian forces in the 1990s (Basic-Palkovic, 2015).

But the Regiment was apparently somewhat picky about who it would even consider allowing into its ranks from western countries. "Every day I receive dozens of requests to join us by e-mail, especially from countries like Finland, Norway and Sweden," Besson said in 2014 (Biloslavo, 2014). "I reject 75 percent of them. We do not want trigger-happy fanatics, drug addicts or alcoholics," he added, noting that potential foreign recruits not only had to pay their own way to Ukraine, but take part in extensive training before getting anywhere near the frontlines.

After the second Minsk agreement in February 2015, things would get even more difficult for foreign fighters who wanted to join Azov's ranks. In those agreements it was stated that foreign units and fighters could no longer be on Ukrainian territory, a statement targeted more at the Russian-led forces than anyone else. While any observer of the war knows the Minsk agreements have hardly been observed to the letter, the statements about withdrawing foreign fighters were apparently taken seriously enough on the Ukrainian side. Since 2015 it has become much more difficult, though not impossible, for a foreigner to serve in Ukraine's armed forces at all, let alone in the Azov Regiment. While the topic of foreign far-right extremists fighting in Ukraine would rear its head again a few years later—a topic I discuss later in this chapter—by 2015 the Regiment proper didn't appear to have too much interest in foreigners who wanted to join their ranks, let alone in forming international friendships. The same can't be said, however, for the broader movement that soon took shape around the regiment, especially National Corps and its international secretary.

Networks and 'new nationalism'

It was a term I'd hear and read more than once: "we are new nationalists," Olena Semenyaka told me in 2018. In her thirties, Semenyaka is pursuing a doctorate in philosophy in Kyiv and is officially the international secretary of National Corps. She is one of the relatively few senior figures in the Azov movement with fluency in a language other than Russian and Ukrainian: in her case, both English and German. Her pre-Maidan biography is more curious; she was part of Russian far-right philosopher Aleksandr Dugin's Eurasianist movement, but broke with him after the revolution and the start of war in 2014 over Dugin's vocal support of Vladimir Putin. While Semenyaka no longer has anything to do with Dugin, her writing style—ranging from the wooden and rambling to the obscurantist and incomprehensible—is reminiscent enough of Dugin's own prose to make one think he has had a lasting influence on her.

In these articles, interviews and social media posts, Semenyaka has made pains to stress that, unlike what she sees as considers the more narrow-minded, 'chauvinistic' nationalism often exercised on the Ukrainian and international far right, the Azov movement subscribes to a 'new nationalism' in the international arena. This so-called new nationalism, in Semenyaka's telling, is focused on overcoming historical differences between European countries and ethnic groups to build a new, united and reborn Europe.

Ukraine and eastern Europe more broadly, in Semenyaka's view, is the perfect place where this rebirth of Europe can begin, a place of stark opposition to the apparent decay and decadence of western Europe. The east is where the claimed true heart of Europe beats and where, as Semenyaka claimed in a 2019 YouTube video, "the region where [European] ethnocultural values are objectively preserved" better than anywhere else on the continent. Thus eastern Europe and particularly Ukraine, owing to the opportunity offered by the war, is an ideal platform for a 'Reconquista,' a term obviously evoking the expulsion of Muslims from the Iberian peninsula hundreds of years ago. The ultimate aim isn't just the defence and rebirth of Ukraine but, in Semenyaka's words, the defence of "the white race" (quoted in Kuzmenko, 2019).

There's nothing new at all about so-called new nationalism, and a trip around Europe's far right shows Azov is hardly alone in thinking this way. Semenyaka's own stated ideological influences, including Nouvelle Droite figures like Guillaume Faye, wrote about the need to form international far-right alliances and overcome historical differences to build a new Europe, a "Europe of a thousand flags" (Griffin, 2014) to resist both American capitalism from the west and Soviet communism from the east. The contemporary European far right is full of people who stress the need to overcome division, from Hungary's neo-Nazi Legio Hungaria to Croatian-American white supremacist Tomislav Sunić. It extends to the online world of Telegram, where pictures with phrases like 'No more brother wars!' with flags of 'traditional' foes, like Serbia and Croatia, will remind those on the far right that unity of Europeans – the white race – must take precedence. This far-right Europe, of course, would be no home for minorities like Jews, Roma and immigrants of non-European background and their descendants. How exactly the advocates of these grandiose far-right visions of the world plan on accounting for the existence of these minorities without resorting to at least some level of ethnic cleansing or outright genocide remains an unanswered question.

Grandiose or not, the Azov movement's international efforts have had several key planks. One of them is Intermarium, whose 2019 conference was planned for Zagreb. Meaning 'between the seas,' the concept of Intermarium has its roots in interwar Poland, where leader Jozef Pilsudski proposed an alliance of central and eastern European countries – similar to the Polish-Lithuanian Commonwealth of centuries before – as a counterweight to both rising Soviet power in the east and German domination in the west. While Pilsudski's plans never saw anything near the light of day, the concept of Intermarium has continued to kick around, even arguably finding some manifestation in the contemporary Three Seas Initiative of central and eastern European countries.

The Azov movement, however, has resurrected a particular vision of Intermarium, an explicitly far-right one that researcher Alexandra Wishart (quoted in Colborne, 2019a) described as a means of neutralizing not just Russian influence but American and EU influence as well. Intermarium is in essence a platform for what Semenyaka described to me as an end goal of "alternative European integration," a springboard for far-right European rebirth. Intermarium's first three conferences in Kyiv, held annually from 2016 to 2018, were attended not only by several far-right figures from across central and eastern Europe, but military attaches from eastern European embassies, including Poland and Hungary, interested in talking about regional defense cooperation. However, the 2020 conference—held online because of the COVID-19 pandemic, and more than a year after the Zagreb conference had been planned—was a much more muted affair, though featured Poland's former ambassador to Ukraine Jan Peklo and other more mainstream figures sharing a virtual platform with speakers from Azov movement leadership.

Given that some its conference attendees over the years have been more mainstream figures with no affiliation to the far right, one might be tempted to paint Intermarium as less an explicitly far-right project than a more mainstream right-wing initiative. But it's evident from Semenyaka's repeated musings on the subject, particularly over 2018 and 2019, that Intermarium has always been a far-right project at its core for her and the Azov Movement. In 2019 Semenyaka publicly described Intermarium as, per her own baffling melange of far-right buzzwords, an "alternative paneuropean (sic) integration within which organic identitarian principles are secured and protected" (Verkkolehti Sarastus, 2019). In that same interview Semenyaka also spoke fondly of the Nouvelle Droite's Guillaume Faye and his theories of Intermarium, and stated that her and her allies' task was "to continue elaborating [Faye's] conception in the geopolitical framework of Intermarium." Semenyaka also added that cooperation with right-wing sympathizers who may not see themselves as far right is an explicit component of hers and Azov's strategy for Intermarium, referring to "at the initial stage also cooperating with "mere" reformists of the EU from the Right."

Another plank of Azov's international efforts have functioned under the banner of 'Paneuropa'. Under Semenyaka's watch, the two Paneuropa conferences in 2017 and 2018 were devoted to meeting, and forming relationships between far-right groups and individuals from all across Europe. Attendees at the 2017 and 2018 conference included representatives from Italy's influential far-right CasaPound movement and German neo-Nazis from The Third Way

(*Der Dritte Weg*) and the National Democratic Party (NPD). French far-right extremist Steven Bissuel—convicted of inciting racial hatred and whose subsequent creation, the violent *Bastion Social* movement, was banned by French president Emmanuel Macron in 2019—as well as American white nationalist and ethnic cleansing proponent Greg Johnson were also attendees. In addition to these conferences, Semenyaka made several trips in 2018 and 2019 to meet with far-right groups and give speeches alongside figures like British neo-Nazi Mark Collett at events in Germany, Sweden, Portugal, Croatia and Italy. In January 2020, in an official response[33] to German parliamentarians asking about far-right networks in the country, authorities revealed "a well-known Ukrainian activist" who had traveled to Germany in February 2019 had been under police observation—almost certainly Semenyaka, who traveled to Germany during that time. Other far-right networking has taken place under the guise of the Asgardsrei festival, the neo-Nazi music festival run primarily by Alexey Levkin that, according to Semenyaka's words to me in 2018, was important not just for music and having fun, but for forming connections and relationships. Attendees at Asgardsrei in the past have included violent neo-Nazi figures, including a leader of Atomwaffen Division in the United States (Colborne, 2019d) who in 2021 pleaded guilty to hate crimes.

Some international far-right extremists online have long had praise for the Azov movement. In English-language Telegram channels and chats, some of which have since been taken down by Telegram for violating its Terms of Service, anonymous chatters whose posts and messages are filled with most vile neo-Nazi rhetoric have regularly looked to Azov for inspiration, sharing photos and posts about the movement and the Regiment. However, it's evident that there's a considerable mixing of fact and fiction about Azov on the most extreme fringes of the online far right; many still

---

33 "*Antwort der Bundesregierung auf die Kleine Anfrage der Abgeordneten Dr. Irene Mihalic, Dr. Konstantin von Notz, Monika Lazar, weiterer Abgeordneter under Fraktion BÜNDNIS 90/DIE GRÜNEN*" ("Answer of the federal government to question of the MPs Dr. Irene Mihalic, Dr. Konstantin von Notz, Monika Lazar, and another member of the BÜNDNIS 90/ DIE GRÜNEN parliamentary fraction"), January 23, 2020, https://dserver.bundestag.de/btd/19/167/1916742.pdf.

seem to think it's relatively easy to join the Azov Regiment or other far-right military units in Ukraine to, in the words of one now-closed channel, familiarize oneself with 21st century warfare. For those from the furthest and most violent extremes that come to Ukraine and try this, as I mention briefly below, they're now more likely to find themselves on a plane back home than in a military unit.

By 2020 what was once a proud and completely unhidden effort from the Azov movement, and particularly Semenyaka, to make foreign friends had gone almost completely quiet. Part of the reason for this is because of international media attention from myself and other journalists, whose stories on Azov and its international outreach brought much more negative attention onto the movement than they probably ever expected. But part of the reason why Azov went quiet on the international front has its roots on what happened on the other side of the world in Christchurch, New Zealand on March 15, 2019.

Foreign fighters, facts and fiction

Brenton Tarrant, the Australian terrorist who murdered 51 people in an attack on two New Zealand mosques in March 2019, was well-travelled in the years and months leading up to his crime. Among the dozens of countries he'd been to, as he alluded to in his manifesto, was Ukraine.

Speculation surfaced in the months after the massacre that Tarrant, while in Ukraine, had trained with Azov and acquired some of the skills he needed to carry out an armed terrorist attack from the Ukrainian far right. Just over six months later, this speculation managed to find its way into a letter from dozens of American congressional representatives in that demanded the US State Department designate the "Azov Battalion," among other international far-right groups, as a foreign terrorist organization. In this letter signed by 40 of his congressional colleagues, Rose wrote that Tarrant claimed in his manifesto that he had trained with Azov in Ukraine. This, as I wrote at the time (Colborne, 2019f), was completely and verifiably false—the terrorist had said absolutely no such thing in his manifesto.

Eventually, a royal commission in New Zealand set up to investigate the attacks would state that Tarrant had been to Ukraine once, for three weeks in August and September 2015. This was among dozens of countries he traveled to during that time, including a month in Russia directly afterwards and visits to five countries in the former Yugoslavia. The last time the terrorist's mother saw him before the attacks, he said he wanted to sell everything he owned and move to Ukraine. Still, there's no evidence Tarrant had any contact with the Azov movement or anyone from Ukraine's far right during his time. There's no evidence that he took part in any combat, tactical or military training with Azov in any capacity. If anything at all connects the two, both Tarrant and Azov have made ample use of the neo-Nazi Black Sun symbol and that, as I've discussed previously, some particularly extreme elements of the Azov movement praised Tarrant and his manifesto and shared the livestreamed video of the attacks, as did other far-right extremists around the world. These shared sympathies should be worrisome enough alone without having to resort to spurious claims about 'training' with Azov.

One consequence of the Christchurch terror attacks was that the issue of far-right terrorism finally managed to grab the attention of politicians and policymakers. Particularly in western countries like the United States, the UK, Germany and others, high-profile far-right terror attacks—including El Paso, Texas in August 2019 and the German city of Hanau in February 2020, to name two of the deadliest—forced the issue much higher up the political agenda. The issue certainly hasn't gone away since the Christchurch terrorist was convicted and imprisoned for life in New Zealand in August 2020. In Germany, a dozen men with more than two dozen unregistered weapons were arrested in February 2020 for allegedly planning to commit terrorist attacks against Muslims, migrants and anti-fascists. British authorities have stated that far-right terrorism is the country's fastest-growing threat (White, 2020), and statistics in the US suggest that far-right extremists are behind a surge in US domestic terror incidents to a level not seen in years (O'Harrow et al, 2021).

It's been in this context that Azov's alleged activities have come under even more scrutiny. A month before Max Rose and colleagues sent their letter to the U.S. State Department, the Soufan Center think tank in Washington, DC published a report claiming that Ukraine had become a hub for far-right extremists who flock to the country to gain combat experience. The report noted that, as of 2019, there had been an estimated 17,000 foreign fighters in Ukraine on both sides of the conflict.

But there's far more to this number, which ended up being frequently quoted in coverage of the report, that meets the eye. As the report itself quietly acknowledged, more than 13,000 of these foreign fighters fought on the Russian-backed side, of whom an estimated 12,000 were Russian: 90 percent. There were estimated to be approximately 3,900 foreign fighters on the Ukrainian side: again, the majority—3,000 soldiers, or more than 75 per cent—were also Russians. Taking both sides of the conflict together an estimated 15,000 of the more than 17,000 foreign fighters in the conflict were from Russia (87 percent). Foreign fighters from countries outside the former Soviet Union never made up anything more than a small minority of foreign fighters in Ukraine, and fewer than 1,000 on the Ukrainian side in total. Moreover, these foreign fighters on the Ukrainian side certainly weren't all part of the far right, nor did they all fight for far-right military units like the Azov Regiment, Right Sector or others. While the Soufan Center's report certainly helped make more people beyond Ukraine aware of the Azov movement and its activities, it also helped muddy the waters considerably; the report's context-stripped presentation of the '17,000 foreign fighters' figure, repeated often in the media, has led more than one person to mistakenly assume that there were 17,000 foreign far-right extremists fighting in Ukraine.

Moreover, the way that the issue of foreign fighters in Ukraine was openly conflated in late 2019 and into 2020 with foreign fighters for the so-called Islamic State (ISIS) in Iraq and Syria not only oversimplified the issue but grossly distorted it. "[It's], in some ways, not too different than what you saw with ISIS," one Soufan Center researcher claimed in 2019 (quoted in Seldin, 2019).

Problem is, it's quite different: ISIS attracted more than 40,000 foreign fighters to its ranks (Dworkin, 2019), more than twice that than came to Ukraine. Unlike those fighters in Ukraine—not all of whom were far right or fought for far-right military units—those who came to fight with ISIS came explicitly to fight with an openly terroristic organization that preached terror and took credit for multiple terrorist attacks around the world. Even the worst of Ukraine's far-right organizations, least of all the Azov movement, aren't particularly keen on officially supporting or encouraging international terrorism, though some individuals within these organizations do. Nonetheless, by early 2020 this was a media frame that really seemed to have caught on with international media, particularly American media and others who didn't normally cover either Ukraine or the far right. And it really seemed to have caught on; I remember, in the span of just a few days in early 2020, being contacted by multiple international journalists asking for information about apparent ISIS-like training camps for far-right foreign fighters in Ukraine.

None of this should obscure the fact that there certainly have been foreign far-right fighters in Ukraine—and that, before the onslaught of international media attention began to hound the movement in 2019, the Azov movement had hoped there would be more. Olena Semenyaka told international far-right friends of Azov in a March 2018 interview to a neo-Nazi group that "right now…is not the best time to join Azov," given that it was difficult to for a foreigner to get a residence permit, live in Ukraine and meet the requirements to serve in Ukraine's armed forces. "[But] in the future we hope to create a foreign legion," she added, where "we could announce loud and clear when we seek volunteers." This foreign legion was something that Semenyaka had discussed repeatedly over early 2019, ambitiously stating that it would be led by former Croatian Brigadier General and French Foreign Legion veteran Bruno Zorica. Before that foreign legion could be formed, Semenyaka said in the March 2018 interview, foreigners would soon be able come to week-long camps in Ukraine to learn military skills;

it's unclear whether these camps ever ended up being set up. What is clear is that in 2018 the Azov movement also made efforts to link up with westerners who wanted to come and fight in Ukraine. Norwegian neo-Nazi Joachim Furholm, then in Ukraine, worked with National Corps and tried to recruit foreigners, particularly Americans, to come to Ukraine to "gain some military experience and hopefully be able to send some of these guys back home to pass on their skills and their knowledge" (quoted in Kuzmenko, 2019). He even openly described himself as a "terrorist facilitator" at one point during his stay in Ukraine (quoted in Kuzmenko, 2019).

More recently, there has clearly still been interest from far-right foreigners in wanting to come fight for the Azov Regiment or other far-right military units, whether those plans have been well thought through or not. Craig Lang, an American as of 2021 in Ukraine fighting extradition stateside for allegedly killing a Florida couple, had fought with his fellow American (and fellow alleged murderer) Alex Zwiefelhofer with Right Sector in eastern Ukraine. Jarret William Smith, an American soldier who had mused online about traveling to Ukraine to fight with the Azov Regiment, was charged and convicted in 2020 of distributing bomb-making information online. Two American members of the neo-Nazi Atomwaffen Division (AWD) were deported from Ukraine in 2020, trying not only to form a local branch but join the Azov Regiment to gain combat experience (Miller, 2020).

The Azov movement, as well former foreign fighters with the Regiment, dismiss the notion that they could be linked to terror at all. In the words of a former foreign member of the Regiment, "What terrorism? What threat?" (quoted in Rekawek, 2020). The issue, though, is hardly something that should be dismissed, given that the threat of far-right terrorism isn't going away. We don't yet know what risks, if any, far-right foreign fighters returning from Ukraine pose to their home countries, though as of 2021 none from the Ukrainian side have ever been linked to any terror attacks or plots. One thing we do know is that, moving into the 2020s, the Azov movement has become much less interested in international outreach of any kind, at least officially and publicly.

Mission unaccomplished?

Even before the beginning of the COVID-19 pandemic in early 2020, the Azov movement's once open and proud international presence had already started to fade away. Gone were National Corps international secretary Olena Semenyaka's frequent Facebook posts about who she was meeting with and where she was going—she and other Azov movement figures were banned from the platform altogether in 2020. Gone were her blog posts, speeches and summaries of meetings and conferences with far-right figures from all across Europe; even ones from previous years ended up being deleted, though are still available on internet archives. What had once been a window for international audiences into the world of Azov, for sympathizers and critics alike, had been slammed shut.

Reading through Semenyaka's past social media posts intended for her international far-right audience, as well as past speeches, interviews and other writings that have since been deleted, one wonders if she ever considered that foreign journalists and observers would read them as well. It was remarkably easy for myself and others trace where the Azov's movement's international secretary was going, what far-right events and conferences she was going to—including who spoke alongside her and what they all said there—and with who she and the movement sympathized. In all, it's hard not to look back on Semenyaka's extremely public actions over 2018 and especially 2019 as a massive own goal for her and the movement, given the extent to which her words and actions helped heap negative publicity on Azov.

Despite this, Semenyaka has blamed others for the negative media attention the movement has received. After a Bellingcat article exposed a French far-right extremist's activities at Asgardsrei (Bourdon, 2020), Semenyaka took to Facebook to express her apparent displeasure at her colleagues being too open and public in their extremism: "I am not the one to interfere with your leisure […] but take care about public representation of your motives if you also have political ambitions," she wrote.[34] At some point after my own

[34] An archived version of this post is available at https://archive.vn/rZniQ.

Bellingcat article about Alexey Levkin and Wotanjugend in September 2019, Semenyaka publicly distanced herself from Levkin, and his "provocative" initiatives reportedly undermined Semenyaka's own ambitions (Nonjon, 2020). And while there's certainly some truth in this—hosting a literal night of Hitler worship isn't exactly a gesture of metapolitical subtlety—Semenyaka was perfectly happy working with and speaking highly of Levkin in the past before his actions gathered media attention from myself and other foreign journalists. As well, Semenyaka had no issue working with Denis Kapustin, who helped facilitate some of the movement's international connections (Miller, 2018), and defended Robert Rundo after the violent American neo-Nazi was arrested in 2019 (Colborne, 2019b). Only when holes started getting poked in the curtains separating Azov's backstage from the front stage did she publicly start to try and distance herself from more extreme figures associated with the Azov movement.

In January 2021, Semenyaka managed to make international headlines when a fellowship she had been awarded at Vienna's Institute for Human Sciences (IWM) was withdrawn. While she inexplicably denied that she was a far-right activist despite being on National Corps' senior council and head of the Intermarium initiative at National Corps headquarters—in short, what any reasonable person would call a 'far-right activist'—her fellowship was taken away within 24 hours of the news being made public. The rescinded fellowship at a prestigious institution didn't just hurt her own ambitions, but those of the Azov movement; National Corps wrote on its Telegram afterwards that the rescinding of her fellowship hindered their dialogue with eastern European allies, suggesting that Semenyaka had planned on doing much more than just scholarly work in the Austrian capital. Semenyaka, despite these setbacks, still clearly has some role within the Azov movement— she remains a member of National Corps' central headquarters staff—though has little to no public presence as of late 2021.

Azov's public international outreach and presence has, to say the least, been considerably downsized. The Intermarium conference in December 2020 featured speakers, including far-right figures, from only three countries outside Ukraine—Poland, Croatia and Estonia. Few elements within the Azov movement, official or unofficial, make a habit of burnishing any international connections publicly; even Tradition and Order, with its links through Denis Kapustin to the German far right and an apparent small cell of support in Germany, seems barely noteworthy next to the strides Azov appeared to making before 2019. Semenyaka did appear online at a far-right conference in February 2021 hosted by the youth wing of Estonia's far-right Conservative People's Party of Estonia (EKRE), with fellow speakers that included Tomislav Sunić and far-right Polish politician Janusz Korwin-Mikke among others. Also, as I've mentioned previously, members of Russia's far right continue to come to Ukraine, aided by those Russians already within the Azov movement.

Where do the Azov movement and its once sky-high international ambitions go from here? Governments around the world, including Ukraine's allies like the US, UK and Germany, continue to focus on the issue of far-right extremism and especially far-right terrorism. Given the negative attention the Azov movement has received for its alleged links to far-right foreign fighters there's likely no way anytime soon that the movement, on any organized or official level, is going to do some of what it's done or at least planned in the past. They likely won't open publicized international 'training camps', accept foreigners like Joachim Furholm to help recruit or try to make the 'foreign legion' into a reality. If they plan to restart some of their international outreach activities—or, indeed, if they are already have—they'll likely do so more quietly, subtly and without advertising it as openly as they used to, and will likely make more concerted efforts to avoid any official connections with the most violent extremes of the global far right. Azov may be down in the international arena, but it's too soon to count them out.

Chapter 7: The Future of Azov

Andriy Biletsky was greeting members of his movement outside a central Kyiv police station in August 2021. Wearing not fatigues but a too-tight navy blue polo shirt and brown cargo pants, the Azov leader looked more like a slightly out-of-shape office worker than the intimidating boss of a far-right movement.

One by one, he shook the hands—the forearms, more accurately, using the Azov movement's faux-Roman greeting—of eight movement members who had been released after being temporarily detained. A few hours earlier they'd destroyed a 'Soviet-style' art installation on the street leading from Maidan up towards Ukraine's parliament where dozens of protesters were slain in February 2014 and are today honoured, an installation that was supposed to be part of official Independence Day celebrations.

Afterwards, after they'd all made their way out of the station, Biletsky stood with a microphone in hand. "Glory to Ukraine," he said, sounding a bit tired as he gave a quick, almost perfunctory Azov fist-from-the-chest salute. Biletsky condemned the inclusion of items from the Soviet era like refrigerators and mock 1970s-vintage apartments as part of an art installation—at a place Ukrainians from the pro-EU mainstream to the nastiest far-right fringes view as almost literal hallowed ground.

It was generally a fairly banal scene as far as the Azov movement is concerned. Members detained temporarily by police, a few dozen other members showing up in support as their comrades end up being released after a few hours' flurry of social media activity: none of this is particularly new or that noteworthy for Azov.

But as I saw the 42-year-old Biletsky—a man at least twice the age of a good proportion of the almost all-male Azov movement contingent there—shake forearms and stand up to speak, I saw something else. I saw a leader, a literal old guard not just of the Azov movement but of more than twenty years' time on Ukraine's far right, looking and sounding less inspired than tired. But also I saw part of the movement's new guard looking ready for action, some of whom had surely been part of violent protests just a few days earlier in front of the presidential administration building, hurling projectiles at police surrounded by clouds of reddish flare-fired smoke.

It wasn't something like a glimpse of Azov's future that I saw, like looking into some sort of crystal ball. What I saw was a reminder that, like all far-right movements, Ukraine's Azov movement has a fundamental dilemma it needs to resolve if it is to grow and, in its view, be successful. But Ukraine's authorities, civil society, media and others in the country—as well as Ukraine's international partners—have some tough choices to make too.

Radicalization or entropy?

Around the world, far-right movements and their members increasingly have a choice to make. While the devotees of metapolitics "consider armed resistance as futile under the present circumstances," some of their more radically-minded comrades "are becoming increasingly anxious to go down a more violent path" (Ravndal, 2021). An example of this is Italy's Ordine Nuovo (New Order), a group where some members became impatient with the long march of metapolitics and started carrying out acts of political violence and terror.

One phrase to help conceptualize this choice for the global far right is 'radicalization or entropy.' Historian Robert Paxton (2004) argues that, at a fifth and final stage of fascism long after a fascist movement has taken power, the state must either become more radical (e.g., Nazi Germany) or slip into what Paxton calls a "tepid authoritarianism" in the case of Fascist Italy (2004). Fascism, in Paxton's words (2004), needs "an impression of driving momentum" as well as an "ever-mounting spiral of ever more daring challenges" to sustain itself lest it decay into a stale semblance of what it used to be.

While the term 'radicalization or entropy' is of course drawn out of a very specific context about the development of Fascist states in the previous century, it's one that applies to the dilemma facing Azov and other contemporary far-right movements. Does the movement become more radical—that is, does it try to recapture the same "headlong, inebriating rush forward" (Paxton, 2004) that inspired it years ago—or does it somewhat disorderedly drift from its roots towards a less extreme version of its former self?

'Radicalization' is an often nebulous word that doesn't always mean what we think it does when we see it. Generally speaking, however, I define radicalization here as "a social and psychological transformation whereby an individual increasingly adopts an extremist belief system, regardless if it ultimately results in actual violence or not" (Ahmed and Obaidi, 2020). In the context of this discussion, those within the Azov movement who have or are becoming increasingly radicalized—keeping in mind that they've already likely undergone at least some degree of radicalization—means that they are becoming increasingly committed to extremist beliefs and particularly to the role of violence in bringing about the social and political changes they want to see.

Watching Azov, one appears to see different elements of the movement pushing in different directions. The movement's leaders, particularly Andriy Biletsky, seem content to try and continuously mainstream themselves and become—or at least appear to be—a less extreme version of what they used to be, eschewing open violence and downplaying revolutionary change, at least in the short term.

On the other hand, some elements within Azov seem particularly impatient. For example, those who once preached metapolitics have moved to serving at the front lines to gain at least some 'real world' military experience (and, not coincidentally, are Ordine Nuovo fanboys). When far-right, Azov-linked actors openly offer up combat and tactical training sessions and position themselves as part of "total resistance" in the case of a full-scale Russian invasion, it's hard not to see echoes of Paxton (2004) again: war is "fascism's clearest radicalizing impulse."

Still, the Azov movement's leadership, particularly under National Corps, is not inevitably prone to drift away from its roots as a matter of course. The opportunity, in Biletsky and company's mind, may well come where radical action is necessary—think, for example, of a full-scale Russian invasion, something increasingly feared in Ukraine—where some of the niceties of the less-extreme-seeming frontstage can be discarded. Azov was built on the inebriating rush of war; it needs war, whether metaphorical, rhetorical or literal, in order to survive.

There's no guarantee that the Azov movement as we know it today will stay a unified movement in the future. Under Biletsky's domineering watch, the Azov movement has become a heterogeneous social movement that, while clearly operateing under one consolidated roof, has its own internal factions and frictions. Whether it's members who want more radical action, or the existence of personal power plays (e.g., an alleged conflict between Sergei Korotkikh and Andriy Biletsky), the Azov movement is hardly one happy little far-right family, even if the extent of these disputes and disagreements remain far out of the public eye or even the knowledge of the movement's rank and file. While the past certainly doesn't always predict the future, it's hard not to look at Azov today and see echoes of their forebears in the OUN, when younger, more radical and more violent members of the movement like Stepan Bandera rose up against their older, more staid colleagues. Azov's future, whether it stays as one, fractures into smaller movements or rests somewhere in between, is hard to predict. But to think that it is somehow too big to fail would be a mistake.

As far-right movements around the world including in Ukraine benefit from varying degrees of social acceptance or mainstream toleration, their bases of support broaden to the point where joining the far right has arguably become less stigmatized (Kruglanski, Webber and Koehler, 2019). But does this mean more violence or less violence? On the one hand, given more relatively mainstream individuals within the ranks of the far right, it could mean a reduction in violence. But it could "just as likely legitimize, embolden, and intensify the violent tendencies" on the far right (Kruglanski, Webber and Koehler, 2019). Fortunately, Ukraine has been spared the ugliness of far-right terror attacks that countries like the United States, Germany and New Zealand have seen in recent years. But the existence of a small minority of extremists that increasingly praises violence and prepares for literal battle can't be discounted as a threat, least of all in the context of a still-hot war. If, in a further worst-case scenario, Ukraine were to descend down the road into a pronounced period of turmoil or even another bloody revolution, this violent, radical and well-trained fringe of the far right would be a force to be reckoned with.

Shifting the discourse

The first step in addressing the problem of Ukraine's far right and especially the Azov movement is, of course, to admit that there actually is a problem. Even as some in Ukraine's mainstream have begun in recent years to admit that one exists, there's still a tendency to downplay the far right, to treat it as something foreign and external to the country – that is, to see it solely as a product of Russian meddling. On top of this, there are some in Ukraine's mainstream who will still deny that the far right is a problem at all. There is little hope of adequately addressing the issue of Ukraine's far right, particularly the Azov movement, if it remains under-covered and seldom discussed in depth in Ukrainian media and political discourse.

Addressing the problem involves more than just pointing at the extremes – the far right everywhere has deeper mainstream roots than we might like to admit. Political scientist Cas Mudde (2010) has long argued that the emergence of the contemporary far right is less a pathology of politics, an aberration caused by crisis, than a "pathological normalcy," a radicalization of already-existing mainstream sentiments. Likewise, Mondon and Winter (2020) warn against "an exaggerated focus on the far right in opposition to a rational and righteous centre," against treating the centre – the mainstream – as inherently good and neutral rather than as something with its own tendencies that have helped enable the far right.

In the context of the Azov movement and Ukraine, it's clear that many of the motivating sentiments I outlined in Chapter 2 as underpinning the Azov movement are almost entirely radicalized, extreme versions of those that exist in so-called 'patriotic' mainstream Ukrainian discourse. This includes, for example, the sense of conspiracism and paranoia – for example, that anyone who criticizes Ukraine is somehow linked to the Kremlin – the feeling that there's a need for an educated elite to guide the unintelligent masses (cf. Gorbach, 2020) or the deep sense of being victimized by both international friends and foes (*zrada*, or "betrayal" in Ukrainian, being a common if sometimes ironically used buzzword). Tackling the way the Azov movement and the far right in general is talked about in Ukraine means tackling the way that these more mainstream sentiments are also discussed.

In theory, this could be done through the use of so-called counternarratives against the far right—"messages that...[demystify], deconstruct or delegitimise extremist narratives" (Tuck and Silverman, 2016). However, these are in short supply in Ukraine. Demystifying, deconstructing and delegitimizing Azov's key narratives, their motivating sentiments, requires doing the same to the narratives and sentiments that exist in mainstream Ukrainian discourse. Bluntly put, however, none of this is likely to happen anytime soon in Ukraine. A country still at war, a country with polarized discourse between so-called 'pro-European' and 'pro-Russian' elements, a country still plagued by many of the same issues that led to the 2014 revolution and, above all, a country wrestling with its very identity is not exactly fertile ground for questioning 'patriotic' mainstream assumptions.

Still, counternarratives could help slowly create an environment where the far right slowly becomes a less appealing option for young Ukrainians. Individuals join the far right for, among other reasons, to have a series of psychological needs met, including a desire to be significant, "the desire to matter and have respect" (Kruglanski, Webber and Koehler, 2019). One way individuals can leave the far right, on the other hand, is to become disillusioned with the ability to have those needs met on the far right. As a result, one tactic for countering the far right's influence could be to show to those tempted to join its ranks, as well as those currently within them, that they're better off looking elsewhere to meet those needs outside the far right—and that being part of the far right "extols a heavy price" on their lives due to social cost and stigma (Kruglanski, Webber and Koehler, 2019). However, it would be hard to argue that being part of the far right in Ukraine nowadays extols much of a heavy price, and any sort of environment where this might be the case won't develop overnight.

So how exactly can public discourse in Ukraine about the far right, and particularly the Azov movement, be shifted in any meaningful way in this context? I would argue that a starting point for unpacking the way Azov is discussed in the discourse—to borrow the language above, to demystify, deconstruct and start to delegitimize its core narratives—is the issue of veterans. As I've discussed throughout this book, the Azov movement has fashioned itself as the primary political representatives of Ukraine's hundreds of thousands of military veterans. Azov know the wealth of political capital that comes with being a veteran in contemporary Ukraine—it's why the veteran status of leaders and senior members are played up so frequently and so loudly, even if it's been years since they served on the front lines.

The irony, of course, is that an increasingly large majority of the Azov movement itself aren't veterans at all. Look through the crowd at any National Corps rally and you'll see face after face of mostly young men who were not only barely teenagers when the war started, but have never been anywhere near the war zone. Azov clearly uses the issue of veterans to cloak itself and its activities in a veneer of patriotism to make what they do more presentable for the mainstream. Think of it as a bridge between themselves and whatever credibility they currently have among Ukraine's mainstream—at least enough to insulate themselves from criticism. It's credibility they need. As that bridge wobbles or even washes away, so does much of Azov's credibility.

Of course, it's hardly just a matter of willpower to start talking and writing about Azov in a different way. The fear that many in Ukraine have about writing critically about the Azov movement is very real. Changing the way Azov is talked about in public discourse requires, above all, changing the social and political structures that continue to enable and empower the movement.

Dismantling the structure

Azov would be nowhere near the movement it is today without the broad array of institutional and structural incentives that have helped it along. The process of dismantling these incentive structures is, in principle, key to curbing the influence and power of the Azov movement.

Corruption: it's the issue that Ukrainians, in numerous polls since 2014, have ranked as the number-one problem in the country, an even greater problem than the war in eastern Ukraine. It's something that, while hardly unique to Ukraine, permeates seemingly every part of political and business life in the country. Oligarchs remain powerful enough to, among other things, have members of parliament in their pockets to advocate for their private interests and allegedly pay far-right movements like the Azov movement to protect their assets and promote their interests. Business owners in shady land disputes will exploit notorious corruption in Ukraine's judiciary to try and seize property from their competitors, and will gladly make use of the far right to help them out. As the arrests of members in Kharkiv in August 2021 suggested, the Azov movement also appears to have little compunction about getting involved in alleged criminal schemes, some of which would require some degree of protection or outright involvement from corrupt local officials and law enforcement. Corruption, in short, has allegedly helped line the Azov movement's pockets and given it opportunities that similar movements in other countries could only imagine.

While there do appear to be steps in progress to address some of these issues, enough time watching post-2014 reform efforts fall flat should leave one playing a more wait-and-see game before praising them. Plans to reform the country's notoriously corrupt judiciary as well as Ukraine's KGB-descended security services, the SBU, are in the works as of 2021 (Prince, 2021). Judicial reform, as I mention above, is sorely needed in Ukraine and has been for years—and, of course, is hardly just about the far right, who have long been able to enjoy a considerable degree of impunity. The same goes for reforms of the SBU, a body long alleged to have its own shady links with the far right in Ukraine. However, Ukraine's experience with much-discussed law enforcement reforms under former interior minister Arsen Avakov—which, while it definitely had some successes, fell far short of what was hoped—shows that powerful political figures and political interests still exert enough influence in Ukraine to single-handedly derail reform efforts. So-called 'deoligarchization,' a plan of Volodymyr Zelenskyy's to limit the influence of oligarchs on Ukrainian politics and society, remains not only a plan still in its infancy, but something that Ukraine's American allies publicly acknowledge as "difficult" (Removska, 2021).

With the departure of Arsen Avakov from the interior ministry in July 2021 and the Azov movement's subsequent complaints of "repression" from Zelenskyy's government, are these processes already partly underway? Ukrainian politics, as even the most casual observer quickly comes to learn, is a particularly byzantine world. It's one where the alleged motivations of political leaders are less dissected and analyzed than speculated upon like a soap opera, with the constant feeling that there is often if not always some ulterior motive behind what's happening—and that it's being done for someone else's interests.

Problem is, in contemporary Ukraine this is often the case. In the case of what the Azov movement decries in mid-2021 as "repression"—the arrests of members for being involved in an alleged criminal scheme and of others for trying to break through a police cordon to confront Zelenskyy, among other things—one shouldn't assume that it's part of some sort of sudden new change of heart about cracking down on the far right, the product of a conscious decision to seriously tackle the issue. But if these or future efforts against the Azov movement are done, not for reasons of recognizing the need to confront the far right, but as part of Ukraine's Machiavellian political games—in short, cracking down on Azov only for someone else's private benefit—it will do nothing to tackle the very structures that have helped make Azov what it is. If the Azov movement, for example, is ejected from Cossack House in central Kyiv because of an allegedly shady ownership dispute and not for the simple reason that a far-right movement shouldn't have a three-story social centre off the main square of a country's capital, this could well prove a pyrrhic victory for opponents of the far right. Cracking down on the far right for the wrong reasons helps no one in the end.

Reforms in Ukraine's armed forces would also help curtail the influence of the Azov movement and the far right in general. As Ukraine's key international allies, like the United States, the United Kingdom, Germany and others make efforts to tackle the issue of far-right extremism in their militaries, Ukraine must also follow suit. As I discussed previously, there is clearly at least some organized far-right presence with Ukraine's armed forces—who have accessed training from Ukraine's western allies—and official recognition of the Freikorps unit has given far-right extremists, including those from the Azov movement, an opportunity to get 'real world' combat experience on the front lines of an active war. There should, in principle, be no home for far-right extremism within Ukraine's armed forces or any country's armed forces, let alone an organized far-right presence. While the efforts of Ukraine's allies to combat far-right extremism in their own ranks have certainly been found wanting at times, neither that nor the war with Russian-backed forces can be an excuse for Ukraine's inaction.

The Azov Regiment is probably the only official military unit in the world that was born from a core of far-right extremists and continues to be connected to a broader far-right social movement. Despite unconvincing efforts to separate the two, it's clear that the Azov Regiment is part of the broader Azov movement and should not be treated as something distinct from it. A military unit like the Azov Regiment has no place in a democratic country's armed forces and should be disbanded.

This is no doubt an unpopular position to take in Ukraine—where the Regiment itself is thought of highly because of its efforts during the heights of war in 2014 and 2015—and certainly an unpopular one with the Azov movement, who have spat back vociferously at those who have dared suggest it. But the broader movement derives its legitimacy from the Regiment itself, a Regiment which still honours its fallen soldiers with a ceremony every September, one that Biletsky always plays a lead role, that with its spotlights and chants and torches more than slightly resembles the *Lichtdom* of Nazi rallies in the 1930s. In an ideal scenario, soldiers within the current Regiment who aren't affiliated with far-right organizations or movements would be moved to other military units within the National Guard, or become part of a renamed Regiment with none of the symbolism of Azov. Even just renaming the Regiment with new leadership unconnected to the far right, completely removing the Wolfsangel symbol and others and casting aside the fascistic rituals could alone be a powerful first step in curtailing the power and influence of the Azov movement.

Ukraine's international allies

Ukraine's international allies, particularly the United States and the European Union, continue to provide considerable financial assistance to the country. Since 2014, the EU has provided an estimated €15 billion in grants and loans to Ukraine, and Germany on its own has provided €1.8 billion of assistance since 2014. Across the Atlantic, the United States provides Ukraine with an estimated $400 million of assistance every year (Prince, 2021). In addition, the International Monetary Fund (IMF) has long provided loans to Ukraine, approving a $5 billion loan in 2020 to be disbursed over 18 months. However, these disbursements came with conditions—they were put on hold in 2021 over IMF concerns about the slow pace of reforms.

Those shouldn't be the only sorts of conditions applied to Ukraine's international financial support. One possible way to encourage Ukraine to tackle its far-right problem, particularly the Azov movement, would be to make some funding contingent on specific actions from Ukraine's authorities. Making even relatively small-scale funding contingent on, for example, addressing far-right extremism in the military or placing sanctions and asset freezes against known far-right figures with proven links to violence and criminal behavior. I don't suggest for a second that Ukraine's international backers should turn off the taps to Ukraine. But it would be worthwhile for the international community to consider using its enormous financial leverage to persuade Ukraine's authorities to take action on the far right.

In addition, too often Ukrainian authorities take action against the far right only when there's considerable international pressure to do so. This isn't to denigrate or downplay those within Ukraine, including activists, journalists and researchers, who take on the far right with considerable risk to their own safety. Ukraine's geopolitical and financial dependence on allies like the EU and the United States means that what is said about Ukraine's far right abroad, and particularly in the corridors of power of Ukraine's allies, matters far more than it might for any other country. Would Ukraine's government, for example, made arrests in the case of a Ukraine-based Telegram channel selling translations of Brenton Tarrant's manifesto were it not for New Zealand Prime Minister Jacinda Ardern making a public case about it in 2019? It isn't fair to those from Ukraine that the words and actions of those of us outside the country, or at least not in Ukraine permanently, end up seeming to carry far more weight. Still, privilege in this context is something that must always be acknowledged, but leveraged and not lamented.

Final thoughts

The Azov movement is unlike any other far-right movement in the world. From the time I first started watching this movement closely in late 2018 – making me, as I acknowledged at the beginning of this book, a latecomer – I've watched almost wide-eyed as it acted more brazenly and openly than any far-right movement I'd ever seen before. I couldn't believe the efforts the movement appeared to be making outside Ukraine's borders. I couldn't believe the things its senior members were freely, openly and unabashedly saying online, as if they never expected to be criticized or called out for a single thing.

But, as the years have gone on, I've had to ask myself if the movement I saw when I first began planning to write this book is the same movement I saw when I finished it. Of course, one answer to that question is yes – everything about the Azov movement at its core is the same, because a leopard can't change its spots. But, on the other hand, the answer is 'no'. It's a movement whose ambitions have been dented from media coverage from journalists like myself. It's a movement, like Biletsky appearing in front of a Kyiv police station in August 2021, sometimes looks like it's becoming exhausted with it all. It's a movement that, by the early 2020s, really seems to be questioning itself and what it should be in the future.

But the Azov movement is not going away anytime soon. They may not be in a position to singlehandedly destabilize Ukraine in fulfillment of the worst of the Kremlin's flights of fancy. But the Azov movement's continued presence on Ukraine's social and political scene, even as it remains forever the preserve of a small minority, poses a threat to liberal democracy in Ukraine. Where the Azov movement goes from here isn't just its choice— in Ukraine and beyond, the choice is ours too.

Acknowledgments

I would never have been able to conceptualize, research, draft and finish this book without the support of colleagues, friends and family. Without delving into some overwrought Oscar-style acceptance speech that needs to be cut off by the orchestra, a few thanks are in order.

First, my thanks to the Centre for the Analysis of the Radical Right (CARR), especially Matthew Feldman, William Allchorn, Bethan Johnson and John E. Richardson, for making this book possible.

Without my colleagues current and former at Bellingcat I never would have had the opportunity to start researching and writing about the Azov movement in as much detail as I did. Thanks are thus due in particular to Eliot Higgins, Aric Toler, Oleksiy Kuzmenko and Natalia Antonova.

BIRN (Balkan Investigative Reporting Network) enabled me to pursue an investigation into Azov's international connections in Croatia as part of a Resonant Voices Fellowship in 2019, which would have been impossible without Marija Ristić, Sofija Todorović and Matt Robinson.

Editors over 2019 and 2020 from a variety of other publications gave me the opportunity to write about Ukraine's far right and especially the Azov movement. Heather Souvaine Horn (The New Republic), Omer Benjakob (Haaretz) and Sasha Polakow-Suransky (Foreign Policy) particularly deserve thanks on that front.

A number of people, whether they know it or not, were incredibly helpful in preparing this book. From interviews and repeat conversations to offhand one-time exchanges of messages they may not even remember, from close friends to people I've only spoken to once, this book wouldn't have been possible without them. It's a list that includes, among others, Jelena Subotić, Mark MacKinnon, Alexey Kovalyov, Katharine Quinn-Judge, Thorsten Hindrichs, Jake Hanrahan, Volodymyr Ishchenko, Veronika Melkozerova, Andrew Lohsen, Taras Fedirko, Alisa Sopova, Noah Buyon, Anya Hrytsenko, Ekaterina Sergatskova, Vyacheslav Likhachev, David

Marples, Khatuna Murgulia, Kacper Rekawek, Stephane Siohan, Cynthia Miller-Idriss, Pavel Klymenko, Leonid Ragozin, Alexandra Wishart, Ian Bateson, Sarah Lain, Alexander Clarkson, Matthew Schaaf, Sergey Movchan, Amy Mackinnon, Tamir Bar-On, Aleksandar Brezar, Anna Shamanska, Fabrice Deprez, Sam Sokol, William Risch, Tom Junes, Jane Lytvynenko, Christopher Miller, Zselyke Csaky, Rina Hajdari, James Montague, Maxim Edwards, Natalie Vikhrov, Nina Jankowicz, Nejra Veljan and particularly Una Hajdari.

Many of you mentioned above have tolerated me over the last few years, including my tendency to bring up random stuff about the far right in conversations when absolutely no one has asked for it. You deserve not just my thanks, but my apologies. The same goes to my family: my parents, my sister and brother-in-law, and most of all my niece and nephew who always wonder what Uncle Mike actually does deserve all the thanks in the world not just for their love and support, but for their patience with me.

References

Ahmed, Uzair and Milan Obaidi. "What is radicalization?" Center for Research on Extremism (C-REX), September 7, 2020, https://www.sv.uio.no/c-rex/english/groups/compendium/what-is-radicalization.html.

Andriushchenko, Eduard. "Ukrayinsk'i pravoradykal'ni orhanizatsiyi u konteksti suspil'no-politychnykh protsesiv *(Kinets' 1980-kh-2015 rr.),*" Doctoral dissertation, Zaporizhian National University, 2015.

Balter, Michael. "Mysterious Indo-European Homeland May Have Been in the Steppes of Ukraine and Russia," *Science*, February 13, 2015, https://www.sciencemag.org/news/2015/02/mysterious-indo-european-homeland-may-have-been-steppes-ukraine-and-russia.

Bar-On, Tamir. *Where Have All the Fascists Gone?* Ashgate Publishing, 2007.

Bar-On, Tamir. *Rethinking the French New Right: Alternatives to Modernity*, Routledge, 2013.

Bašić-Palković, Danijela. "Gaston Besson: U AZOV ne primamo fanatike, narkomane, alkoholičare lake na okidaču, internet ratnike, fašiste, nabrijane klince željne krvi," *Novi List*, February 22, 2015, https://www.novilist.hr/novosti/svijet/gaston-besson-u-azov-ne-primamo-fanatike-narkomane-alkoholicare-lake-na-okidacu-internet-ratnike-fasiste-nabrijane-klince-zeljne-krvi/.

Bellingcat Anti-Equality Monitoring. "The Russians and Ukrainians Translating the Christchurch Shooter's Manifesto," *Bellingcat*, August 14, 2019, www.bellingcat.com/news/uk-and-europe/2019/08/14/the-russians-and-ukrainians-translating-the-christchurch-shooters-manifesto/.

Bellingcat Anti-Equality Monitoring. "Ukraine's Ministry of Veterans Affairs Embraced the Far Right - With Consequences to the U.S.," *Bellingcat*, November 11, 2019, https://www.bellingcat.com/news/uk-and-europe/2019/11/11/ukraines-ministry-of-veterans-affairs-embraced-the-far-right-with-consequences-to-the-u-s/.

Bereza, Anastasia. "Andrey Biletskiy. Kak voina prevratila polituznika v komandira batal'ona Azov," *Novoye Vremya*, October 22, 2014, https://nv.ua/publications/andrey-bileckiy-kak-voyna-prevratila-polituznika-v-komandira-batalona-azov-17031.html.

Berezhniuk, Olena. "«Azov» vydaie svoiu «operatyvku»," *Den'*, January 23, 2015, https://day.kyiv.ua/uk/article/media/azov-vydaye-svoyu-operatyvku.

Bezruk, Tetiana. "Ukraine's all-powerful interior minister resigns – and leaves a legacy of impunity behind," *openDemocracy*, July 16, 2021, https://www.opendemocracy.net/en/odr/ukraine-avakov-resignation-impunity/.

Biletsky, Andriy. *Word of the White Leader*, 2013, https://web.archive.org/web/20140924041340/http://rid.org.ua/knigarnya/AB/slovo.pdf.

Biloslavo, Fausto. "Ukraine: Far-Right Fighters from Europe Fight for Ukraine," *Eurasianet*, August 6, 2014, https://eurasianet.org/ukraine-far-right-fighters-from-europe-fight-for-ukraine.

Bilous, Taras, Oleksandr Kravchuk and Roman Huba, "Legislating land reform in Ukraine," Rosa Luxemburg Stiftung, March 2020, https://www.rosalux.de/en/publication/id/41837/legislating-land-reform-in-ukraine.

Bivings, Liliane. "Ukraine's powerful Interior Minister Avakov under fire over police reform failures," *Atlantic Council*, June 30, 2020, https://www.atlanticcouncil.org/blogs/ukrainealert/ukraines-powerful-interior-minister-avakov-under-fire-over-police-reform-failures/.

Blamires, Cyprian and Paul Jackson, ed. *World Fascism: A-K,* ABC-Clio, 2006.

Boichenko, Nina. "Inside Ukraine's ideological renewal," *New Eastern Europe,* October 4, 2017, https://neweasterneurope.eu/2017/10/04/inside-ukraines-ideological-renewal/.

Bourdon, Sébastien. "At Ukraine's Asgardsrei, A French Connection," *Bellingcat,* May 1, 2020, https://www.bellingcat.com/news/2020/05/01/at-ukraines-asgardsrei-a-french-connection/.

Burdyga, Igor. "Chervoni ekskavatornyky: shcho «Azov» robyt' na zavodi «ATEK»," *Hromadske,* April 3, 2018, https://hromadske.ua/posts/shcho-azov-robyt-na-zavodi-atek.

Burdyga, Igor. "Za chto ubili Pavla Sheremeta? Osnovnyye versii," *DW,* January 10, 2021, https://www.dw.com/ru/za-chto-ubili-pavla-sheremeta-osnovnye-versii/a-56162757.

Chernysh, Oleg. "Vdova eks-rukovoditelya "Azova" Babicha nazvala ubiyts muzha i prizvala SBU vozobnovit' rassledovaniye," *Ukraiyins'ki Novyny,* March 15, 2019, https://ukranews.com/news/619917-vdova-eks-rukovoditelya-azova-babicha-nazvala-ubijts-muzha-i-prizvala-sbu-vozobnovit-rassledovanie.

Cherpurko, Valeriya. ""Kto-to ukral nashe imya i ideyu" - predstaviteli organizatsii Centuria oprovergayut prezentatsiyu s maskami i strel'boy," *KP v Ukraine,* August 3, 2020, https://kp.ua/life/673586-kto-to-ukral-nashe-ymia-y-ydeui-predstavytely-orhanyzatsyy-Centuria-oproverhauit-prezentatsyui-s-maskamy-y-strelboi.

Colborne, Michael. "Croatia Key to Ukrainian Far-Right's International Ambitions," *Balkan Insight*, July 18, 2019 (a), https://balkaninsight.com/2019/07/18/croatia-key-to-ukrainian-far-rights-international-ambitions/.

Colborne, Michael. "Friday Night Fights with Ukraine's Far Right," *The New Republic*, July 9, 2019 (b), https://newrepublic.com/article/154434/friday-night-fights-ukraines-far-right.

Colborne, Michael. "Inside The Extremist Group That Dreams of Ruling Ukraine," *Haaretz*, February 23, 2019 (c), https://www.haaretz.com/world-news/europe/.premium-inside-the-extremist-group-that-dreams-of-ruling-ukraine-1.6936835.

Colborne, Michael. "Most neo-Nazi Music Festivals Are Closely Guarded Secrets – Not This One in Ukraine," *Haaretz*, December 12, 2019 (d), https://www.haaretz.com/world-news/europe/.premium-most-neo-nazi-music-festivals-are-closely-guarded-secrets-not-this-one-1.8260218.

Colborne, Michael. "This Jewish Comedian Is About To Become Ukraine's President – No Joke," *The Forward*, April 17, 2019 (e), https://forward.com/news/422050/jewish-comedians-pogrom-ukraine/.

Colborne, Michael. "U.S. Congress Accidentally Boosted Ukraine's Far-Right," *Foreign Policy*, November 1, 2019 (f), https://foreignpolicy.com/2019/11/01/congress-max-rose-ukraine-azov-terrorism/.

Colborne, Michael. "Ukraine's Far Right Is Boosting A Pro-Putin Fascist," *Bellingcat*, January 22, 2020, https://www.bellingcat.com/news/2020/01/22/ukraines-far-right-is-boosting-a-pro-putin-fascist/.

Colborne, Michael. "What links organised crime with the radical right?," *openDemocracy*, July 16, 2021, https://www.opendemocracy.net/en/countering-radical-right/what-links-organised-crime-radical-right/.

Colborne, Michael and Oleksiy Kuzmenko. "The 'Hardcore' Russian Neo-Nazi Group That Calls Ukraine Home," *Bellingcat*, September 4, 2019, https://www.bellingcat.com/news/uk-and-europe/2019/09/04/the-hardcore-russian-neo-nazi-group-that-calls-ukraine-home/.

Coynash, Halya. "BORN in the Kremlin? Russian ultranationalist trial and links with Ukraine," Kharkiv Human Rights Protection Group, June 12, 2015, https://khpg.org/en/1433976348.

Coynash, Halya. "Russia's fake 'Ukrainian fascist' returns to Ukraine to fight against 'fratricidal' war in Donbas," Kharkiv Human Rights Protection Group, August 12, 2020, https://khpg.org/en/1596991069.

Coynash, Halya. "Belarusian activist threatened with deportation from Ukraine for criticizing the police," Kharkiv Human Rights Protection Group, July 20, 2021, https://khpg.org/en/1608809344.

Curry, Andrew. "Europe's Languages Were Carried From the East, DNA Shows," *National Geographic*, March 3, 2015, https://www.nationalgeographic.com/culture/article/150303-human-dna-europe-language-archaeology.

Deprez, Fabrice. "Ukraine's ultranationalists have no presidential candidate. But they're still at the polls." *PRI*, March 28, 2019, https://www.pri.org/stories/2019-03-28/ukraine-s-ultranationalists-have-no-presidential-candidate-they-re-still-polls.

Dorell, Oren. "Volunteer Ukrainian unit includes Nazis," *USA Today*, March 10, 2015, https://www.usatoday.com/story/news/world/2015

/03/10/ukraine-azov-brigade-nazis-abuses-separatists/24664937/.

Dumskaya, "Ne natsionalisty, a konservatory: kto na samom dele stoit za napadeniyem na odesskiy «Marsh ravenstva»," August 30, 2020, https://dumskaya.net/news/ne-natcionalisty-a-konservatory-kto-stoit-za-nap-124104/.

Dworkin, Anthony. "Beyond good and evil: Why Europe should bring ISIS foreign fighters home," European Council on Foreign Relations, October 25, 2019, https://ecfr.eu/publication/beyond_good_and_evil_why_europe_should_bring_isis_foreign_fighters_home/.

Eatwell, Roger. "Towards a New Model of Generic Fascism," *Journal of Theoretical Politics* 4 (1992):162, 172–174._

Eatwell, Roger. "Ten theories of the extreme right," In P. Merkl, & L. Weinberg (Eds.), *Right-Wing Extremism in the Twenty-first Century* (pp. 45-70), Frank Cass, 2003.

Fanailova, Elena. ""Ya znayu, kto uchastvoval v ubiystve,"" *Radio Svoboda,* November 27, 2016, https://www.svoboda.org/a/28131520.html.

Fedorenko, Konstantyn and Andreas Umland. "Between front and parliament: links among Ukrainian political parties and irregular armed groups in 2014-2019," Ideology and Politics Journal, 2(16), 2020.

Feldman, Matthew. "Between 'Geist' and 'Zeitgeist': Martin Heidegger as Ideologue of Metapolitical Fascism," In *Politics, Intellectuals and Faith,* ibidem-Verlag/Columbia University Press, 2020.

Feldman, Matthew and Paul Jackson. "Introduction," in M. Feldman, and P. Jackson (eds.) *Doublespeak. The Rhetoric of the Far Right since 1945,* Ibidem Verlag, 2014.

Feshchenko, Ihor, Nataliia Patrikieieva, and Vita Dumanska. "Hroshi "Natskorpusu": skhema chy tysiachi viddanykh partiytsiv?" Chesno, May 18, 2020. https://www.chesno. org/post/3987/.

Fraza. "«Azov» zanimayetsya maroderstvom i grabezhami. Batal'on prevratilsya v bandu, tuda prinimayut tol'ko krayne pravykh /Yaroslav Gonchar/," June 25, 2014, https://fraza.com /news/199702-%C2%ABazov%C2%BB_zanimaetsja_maroderstvom_i_grabezhami_batalon_prevratilsja_v_bandu_tuda_prinimajut_tolko_krajne_pravyh_jaroslav_gonchar.

Fraza. "Natsionalisty pytalis' zakhvatit' TTS na okraine Kieva," December 11, 2018, https://fraza.com/video/274375-natsionalisty-pytalis-zahvatit-tts-na-okraine-kieva.

Friedrich, Julia and Theresa Lütkefend. "The Long Shadow of Donbas: Reintegrating Veterans and Fostering Social Cohesion in Ukraine," Global Public Policy Institute/Konrad-Adenauer-Stiftung, May 10, 2021, https://www.gppi.net/2021/05/10/the-long-shadow-of-donbas.

Furmaniuk, Artem. "Komandyr "Azovu" fihuruie u spravi pro pohrabuvannia inkasatoriv "Oshchadbanku," *Resonance.ua,* August 11, 2016, https://resonance.ua/artem-furmanyuk-komandir-azovu-figuruye-u-spravi-pro-pograbuvannya-inkasatoriv-oshhadbanku/.

Furmaniuk, Artem. "Avakov pokryvayet ubiyts? «Azov» i rezonansnyye ubiystva v Ukraine: sovpadeniy slishkom mnogo," *Argument,* December 25, 2017, http://argumentua.com/stati/avakov-pokryvaet-ubiits-azov-i-rezonansnye-ubiistva-v-ukraine-sovpadenii-slishkom-mnogo.

Gaubert, Julie. "Protests in Kyiv over allowing the sale of Ukraine's prized farmland," *AFP,* December 17, 2019, https://www.euronews.com/2019/12/17/protests-in-kyiv-over-allowing-the-sale-of-ukraine-s-farmland.

Gerashchenko, Anton. "13 iyunya - den' osvobozhdeniya Mariupolya!" [Facebook post], June 12, 2015, https://archive.vn/tTJ5q.

Gerashchenko, Anton. "Vchera ispolnilos' rovno dva goda s momenta prinyatiya resheniya o sozdanii stavshego uzhe legendarnym batal'ona "Azov"" [Facebook post], May 6, 2016, https://archive.vn/3X5Ah.

Glavcom. "Sim'ia komandyra «Azova» Bilets'koho pid chas boyiv za donets'kyi aeroport kupyla kvartyru v stolytsi," May 23, 2016, https://glavcom.ua/news/simya-komandira-azova-bileckogo-pid-chas-bojiv-za-doneckiy-aeroport-kupila-kvartiru-v-stolici-352633.html.

GolosUA. "Boytsy «Azova» uchastvuyut v reyderskom zakhvate predpriyatiya na Poltavshchine," July 31, 2018, https://golos.ua/news/bojtsy-azova-uchastvuyut-v-rejderskom-zahvate-predpriyatiya-na-poltavshhine.

Gomza, Ivan, and Johann Zajaczkowski. "Black Sun Rising: Political Opportunity Structure Perceptions and Institutionalization of the Azov Movement in Post-Euromaidan Ukraine," *Nationalities Papers* 47, no. 5 (2019): 774–800. doi:10.1017/nps.2019.30.

Gontar, Marina. "Den'gi ne pakhnut: byvshiy osnovatel' «Azova» rasskazal, kak Akhmetov nanimal boytsov batal'ona dlya okhrany i silovoy podderzhki," *Klymenko Time*, January 8, 2021, https://klymenko-time.com/novosti/dengi-ne-pahnut-byvshij-osnovatel-azova-rasskazal-kak-ahmetov-nanimal-bojczov-batalona-dlya-ohrany-i-silovoj-podderzhki-mago/ 2021

Goodrick-Clarke, Nicholas. *Black Sun: Aryan Cults, Esoteric Nazism and the Politics of Identity*. New York University Press, 2002.

Gorbach, Denys. "Entrepreneurs of political violence: the varied interests and strategies of the far-right in Ukraine," *openDemocracy*, October 16, 2018, https://www.opendemocracy.net/en/odr/entrepreneurs-of-political-violence-ukraine-far-right/.

Gorbach, Denys. "Middle class populism in Ukraine: looking for the "real people"," *openDemocracy*, July 9, 2020, https://www.opendemocracy.net/en/odr/middle-class-populism-in-ukraine-looking-for-the-real-people/.

Griffin, Roger. *The Nature of Fascism*, Pinter Publishers Ltd., 1991.

Griffin, Roger. "The Primacy of Culture: The Current Growth (or Manufacture) of Consensus within Fascist Studies." Journal of Contemporary History 37, no. 1 (January 2002): 21–43. https://doi.org/10.1177/00220094020370010701.

Griffin, Roger. "Fascism's New Faces (and New Facelessness) in the 'post-fascist' Epoch." In: Feldman, Matthew (ed) *A Fascist Century*, Palgrave Macmillan, 2008, https://doi.org/10.1057/9780230594135_8.

Griffin, Roger. "Lingua Quarti Imperii. The Euphemistic Tradition of Extreme Right." In M. Feldman, and P. Jackson (eds.) *Doublespeak. The Rhetoric of the Far Right since 1945*, Ibidem Verlag, 2014.

Grinberg, Myroslav. "Symboly Nenavysti," Ukrainian Helsinki Committee, 2021, https://helsinki.org.ua/wp-content/uploads/2021/02/Prev-Hate_Symbols_A4.pdf.

Haak, Wolfgang, Iosif Lazaridis, Nick Patterson, Nadin Rohland, Swapan Mallick, Bastien Llamas, Guido Brandt et al. "Massive Migration from the Steppe Was a Source for Indo-European Languages in Europe." *Nature* 522, no. 7555 (June 2015): 207–11. https://doi.org/10.1038/nature14317.

Hajdari, Una. "How Russia and Rising Nationalism Are Defeating Anti-fascism in Europe," *Haaretz*, May 13, 2020, https://www.haaretz.com/world-news/.premium-how-russia-is-helping-defeat-anti-fascism-in-europe-1.8842513.

Halikiopolou, Daphne. "'Far right' groups may be diverse – but here's what they all have in common," *The Conversation*, September 27, 2018, https://theconversation.com/far-right-groups-may-be-diverse-but-heres-what-they-all-have-in-common-101919.

Himka, John-Paul. "The Organization of Ukrainian Nationalists and the Ukrainian Insurgent Army: Unwelcome Elements of an Identity Project," *Ab Imperio*. 2010. 83-101. 10.1353/imp.2010.0101.

Himka, John-Paul. "Shche kil'ka sliv pro l'vivs'kyy pohrom," *Istorychna Pravda,* February 25, 2013, https://www.istpravda.com.ua/columns/2013/02/25/114048/.

Hlukohavskyi, Mykhailo and Stanislav Gruzdev. "Komandyr «Natsional'nykh druzhyn» Ihor Mykhailenko: ya siv u tiurmu u 23 roky, navit' ne zakinchyvshy instytut," *Glavcom*, February 23, 2018, https:// glavcom.ua/interviews/komandir-nacionalnih-druzhin-igor-mihaylenko-ya-siv-u-tyurmu-u-23-roki-navit-ne-zakinchivshi-institut-475803.html.

Hromadske. "Zemlya chy hroshi—chomu zahynuv zasnovnyk «Azova» Yaroslav Babych?" August 10, 2016, https://hromadske.radio/podcasts/hromadska-hvylya/zemlya-chy-groshi-chomu-zagynuv-zasnovnyk-azova-yaroslav-babych.

Ishchenko, Volodymyr. "Insufficiently Diverse: The Problem of Nonviolent Leverage and Radicalization of Ukraine's Maidan Uprising, 2013–2014." Journal of Eurasian Studies 11, no. 2 (July 2020): 201–15. https://doi.org/10.1177/1879366520928363.

Ivanov, Hlib. ""Titushky", vybukhy i deputats'kyy "dakh": yak reyderyly rynok "Stolychnyi,"" *Obozrevatel,* May 24, 2021, https://news.obozrevatel.com/ukr/kiyany/titushki-vibuhi-i-deputatskij-dah-yak-rejderili-rinok-stolichnij.htm.

Jacobson, Roni. "New Evidence Fuels Debate over the Origin of Modern Languages," *Scientific American*, March 1, 2018, https://doi.org/10.1038/scientificamerican0318-12.

Jamieson, Alastair. "Mafia crook among 19 suspects in plot to create new Nazi party in Italy," *Euronews*, November 28, 2019, https://www.euronews.com/2019/11/28/mafia-crook-among-19-suspects-in-plot-to-create-new-nazi-party-in-italy.

Johnson, Greg. "Restoring White Homelands," *Counter-Currents*, June 24, 2014, https://archive.ph/C0fiz.

Jupskås, Anders Ravik and Iris Beau Segers. "What is right-wing extremism?" Center for Research on Extremism (C-REX), August 31, 2020, https://www.sv.uio.no/c-rex/english/groups/compendium/what-is-right-wing-extremism.html.

Kondratova, Valeriia. "C14. Kto oni i pochemu im pozvoleno bit' lyudey," *Liga.net*, November 15, 2017, https://news.liga.net/politics/interview/s14_kto_oni_i_pochemu_im_pozvoleno_bit_lyudey.

Koshkina, Sonia. "Andriy Bilets'kyy: «Parlament treba perezavantazhuvaty. Yaknayshvydshe»," *Levyi Bereh*, February 21, 2018, https://lb.ua/news/2018/02/21/390730_andriy_biletskiy_parlament_treba.html.

Kovalenko, Kateryna. "Ne khodiat' na vybory, khochut' nosyty zbroiu, pokhovaly feminizm u truni. Khto taki «Sriblo troiandy» – velykyy profayl orhanizatsiyi," *Babel'*, March 17, 2020, https://babel.ua/texts/40616-ne-hodyat-na-vibori-hochut-nositi-zbroyu-pohovali-feminizm-u-truni-hto-taki-sriblo-troyandi-velikiy-profayl-organizaciji.

Krakowsky, Lelik, "'Revanche': Opposition Nationalists Pledge Their Cooperation with the Authorities (Part 1)," *Reft & Light*, October 31, 2016, http://reftlight.euromaidanpress.com/2016/10/31/revanche-opposition-nationalists-pledge-their-cooperation-with-the-authorities-part-1/.

Kruglanski, Arie, W., David Webber and Daniel Koehler. *The Radical's Journey*. Oxford University Press, 2019.

Kulichenko, Ivan. ""Azov" zvynuvatyv Odnorozhenka u brekhni," *Strayk,* June 11, 2018, https://web.archive.org/web/20180614120336/http:/firstsocial.info/news/azov-zvinuvativ-odnorozhenka-u-brehni.

Kupfer, Matthew. "Yes, That's Rudy Giuliani in Kharkiv. But Why?" *The Odessa Review*, November 21, 2017, http://odessareview.com/yes-thats-rudy-giuliani-kharkiv/.

Kuzmenko, Oleksiy and Michael Colborne. "Ukrainian Far-Right Extremists Receive State Funds to Teach "Patriotism,"" *Bellingcat*, July 16, 2019, https://www.bellingcat.com/news/uk-and-europe/2019/07/16/ukrainian-far-right-extremists-receive-state-funds-to-teach-patriotism/.

Kuzmenko, Oleksiy. ""Defend the White Race": American Extremists Being Co-Opted by Ukraine's Far-Right," *Bellingcat*, February 15, 2019, https://www.bellingcat.com/news/uk-and-europe/2019/02/15/defend-the-white-race-american-extremists-being-co-opted-by-ukraines-far-right/.

Kuzmenko, Oleksiy. "The Azov Regiment has not depoliticized," *Atlantic Council*, March 19, 2020, https://www.atlanticcouncil.org/blogs/ukrainealert/the-azov-regiment-has-not-depoliticized/.

Kuzmenko, Oleksiy. "Far-Right Group Made Its Home in Ukraine's Major Western Military Training Hub," Institute for European,

Russian, and Eurasian Studies (IERES), The George Washington University, September 21, 2021, https://www.illiberalism.org/far-right-group-made-its-home-in-ukraines-major-western-military-training-hub/.

Lelych, Milan. "Komandir "Azova" Andrey Biletskiy: U natsionalistov na fronte proizoshla evolyutsiya vzglyadov," *Fokus*, October 23, 2014, https://focus.ua/politics/318261.

Likhachev, Vyacheslav. "Chto NAM v NIKH ne nravitsya-I: Andrey Biletskiy," *Etnograficheskoye oborzeniye*, November 5, 2014, https://corneliu.livejournal.com/227914.html.

Likhachev, Vyacheslav. "The "right sector" and others: The behavior and role of radical nationalists in the Ukrainian political crisis of late 2013 – Early 2014," *Communist and Post-Communist Studies*, 2015, 48(2–3), 257–271.

Likhachev, Vyacheslav. "Far-right Extremism as a Threat to Ukrainian Democracy," *Freedom House*, May 2018, https:// freedomhouse.org/report/analytical-brief/2018/far-right-extremism-threat-ukrainian-democracy.

Likhachev, Vyacheslav. "Democracy Study Centre 2018: Lecture by Viacheslav Likhachev," *YouTube*, December 20, 2018 (b), https://www.youtube.com/watch?v=4ob1eu7uziw&t=5260s.

Luchistaya, Alyona. "Po faktu napadeniya na «MK» vozbuzhdeno ugolovnoye delo," *Novyi Den'*, July 16, 2013, https://archive.ph/oANSr.

McBride, Jared. "Peasants into Perpetrators: The OUN-UPA and the Ethnic Cleansing of Volhynia, 1943–1944." *Slavic Review* 75, no. 3 (2016): 630–54. doi:10.5612/slavicreview.75.3.0630.

Miller-Idriss, Cynthia. *The Extreme Gone Mainstream: Commercialization and Far Right Youth Culture in Germany,* Princeton University Press, 2019.

Miller, Christopher. "Justice Denied," Committee to Protection Journalists (CPJ), 2017, https://cpj.org/reports/2017/07/justice-denied-ukraine-pavel-sheremet-murder-probe-journalist-about/.

Miller, Christopher. "Azov, Ukraine's Most Prominent Ultranationalist Group, Sets Its Sights On U.S., Europe," *Radio Free Europe/Radio Liberty*, November 14, 2018, https://www.rferl.org/a/azov-ukraine-s-most-prominent-ultranationalist-group-sets-its-sights-on-u-s-europe/29600564.html.

Miller, Christopher. "G7 Letter Takes Aim At Role Of Violent Extremists In Ukrainian Society, Election," *Radio Free Europe/Radio Liberty*, March 22, 2019, https://www.rferl.org/a/g7-takes-aim-at-role-of-violent-extremists-in-ukrainian-society-election/29836811.html.

Miller, Christopher. "Ukraine Deported Two American Members Of A Neo-Nazi Group Who Tried To Join A Far-Right Military Unit For "Combat Experience"," *BuzzFeed News*, October 8, 2020, https://www.buzzfeednews.com/article/christopherm51/ukraine-deports-american-neo-nazi-atomwaffen-division.

Ministry of Youth and Sports, Ukraine. "Government adopted the first in Ukraine state targeted social program of national-patriotic education for the period up to 2025," June 30, 2021, https://www.kmu.gov.ua/en/news/uryad-zatverdiv-pershu-v-ukrayini-derzhavnu-cilovu-socialnu-programu-nacionalno-patriotichnogo-vihovannya-na-period-do-2025-roku.

Mondon, Aurelien and Aaron Winter. "From demonization to normalization: Reflecting on far right research." In *Researching the Far Right: Theory, Method and Practice*, eds. S. Ashe, J. Busher, G. Macklin, and A. Winter, Routledge, 2020.

Mondon, Aurelien. "Objectivity, impartiality and neutrality in researching the far right," In *The Ethics of Researching the Far Right*, conference contribution, 2020.

Montague, James. "*1312: Among the Ultras: A Journey with the World's Most Extreme Fans,*" Ebury press, 2020.

Mudde, Cas. *The Ideology of the Extreme Right*, Manchester University Press, 2000.

Myachina, Katya. "Conflicts and Militarization of Education: Totalitarian Institutions in Secondary Schools and in the System of Extracurricular Education in Ukraine (Part 3)," *Journal of Conflict Transformation*, April 15, 2020, https://caucasusedition.net/conflict-and-militarization-of-non-formal-education-in-ukraine-part-3/.

National Corps. ""Tse lyudyna chasiv Velykoyi viyny, yaka dotorknulasya do vichnoho", – Andriy Bilets'kyy pro Ernsta Yunhera na prezentatsiyi knyhy," January 23, 2019, https://archive.ph/XArRi.

Neaman, Elliot. "Ernst Jünger and Storms of Steel." In *Key Thinkers of the Radical Right: Behind the New Threat to Liberal Democracy*, edited by Mark Sedgwick, Oxford University Press, 2019, doi: 10.1093/oso/9780190877583.003.0002.

Nedelia. "Molodi Biytsi," March 11, 2020, https://nedelya.info/news/item/11138-molodi-bijtsi.

Newman, Dina. "Ukraine conflict: 'White power' warrior from Sweden," *BBC News*, July 16, 2014, https://www.bbc.com/news/world-europe-28329329.

Nonjon, Adrien. "Olena Semenyaka, The "First Lady" of Ukrainian Nationalism," Institute for European, Russian, and Eurasian

Studies (IERES), The George Washington University, October 20, 2020, https://www.illiberalism.org/olena-semenyaka-the-first-lady-of-ukrainian-nationalism/.

NovyNarnia, ""Vidchynyayut'sia dveri – mene z liktia b"yut' u holovu," Veteran "Azovu" Filimonov rozpoviv, yak iz nym "rozmovlyaly" partiytsi," May 9, 2020, https://novynarnia.com/2020/05/09/filimonov/.

O'Harrow Jr, Robert, Andrew Ba Tran and Derek Hawkins. "The rise of domestic extremism in America," *Washington Post,* April 12, 2021, https://www.washingtonpost.com/investigations/interactive/2021/domestic-terrorism-data/.

Office of the United Nations High Commissioner for Human Rights. "Report on the human rights situation in Ukraine 16 February to 15 May 2016," June 3, 2016, https://www.ohchr.org/Documents/Countries/UA/Ukraine_14th_HRMMU_Report.pdf.

Olszański, Tadeusz A. "Svoboda party – the new phenomenon on the Ukrainian right-wing scene," Centre for Eastern Studies (OSW), May 7, 2011, https://www.osw.waw.pl/en/publikacje/osw-commentary/2011-07-05/svoboda-party-new-phenomenon-ukrainian-right-wing-scene.

Onuch, Olga. "EuroMaidan Protests in Ukraine: Social Media Versus Social Networks," *Problems of Post-Communism,* 62:4, 217-235, DOI: 10.1080/10758216.2015.1037676

Onuch, Olga and Gwendolyn Sasse. "The Maidan in Movement: Diversity and the Cycles of Protest," *Europe-Asia Studies,* 68:4, 556-587, 2016, DOI: 10.1080/09668136.2016.1159665.

Orwell, George. *Nineteen Eighty-Four*. Secker & Warburg, 1949.

Ostrogniew, Jarosław. "Przeciwko wszystkim: Asgardsrei 2019 (Kijów, 13-15.12.2019)," *Szturm!* December 31, 2019, https://archive.ph/CDRQb.

Passmore, Kevin. *Fascism: A Very Short Introduction (1st edn)*. Oxford University Press, 2002.

Perevozkina, Marina. "Boytsy ukrainskogo «Azova» nachali unichtozhat' drug druga: klub samoubiyts," *MK*, June 6, 2021, https://www.mk.ru/politics/2021/06/06/boycy-ukrainskogo-azova-nachali-unichtozhat-drug-druga-klub-samoubiyc.html.

Petik, Oles and Gorbach, Denys. "The rise of Azov," *openDemocracy*, February 15, 2016, https://www.opendemocracy.net/en/odr/rise-of-azov/.

Philip, Rowan. "Tips for Investigating Far Right Groups Around the World," Global Investigative Journalism Network (GIJN), March 3, 2021, https://gijn.org/2021/03/03/tips-for-investigating-far-right-groups-around-the-world/.

Plokhy, Serhii. *The Gates of Europe: A History of Ukraine*. Basic Books, 2015.

Polishchuk, Ihor and Oleksiy Suvorov. "Andriy Bilets'kyy: kolyshnikh «Azovtsiv» ne buvaie!" *Willlive*, February 20, 2019, https://archive.ph/Kupch.

Ponomarenko, Illia. "After years in limbo, SBU reform makes slow headway," *Kyiv Post*, July 26, 2021, https://www.kyivpost.com/ukraine-politics/after-years-in-limbo-sbu-reform-makes-slow-headway.html.

Poragovorit. "Khar'kovskiye natsionalisty «otmetilis'» melkoy krazhey v Danii," January 11, 2019, https://poragovorit.com/news/42810-harkovskie-nacionalisty-otmetilis-melkoy-krazhey-v-danii.html.

Portnov, Andrii. "Bandera mythologies and their traps for Ukraine," *openDemocracy*, June 22, 2016, https://www.opendemocracy.net/en/odr/bandera-mythologies-and-their-traps-for-ukraine/.

Povorozniuk, Oleksandar. "Zemel'noyi reformy boyat'sia ti, khto proplachuye mitynhy," *Stopkor,* February 11, 2020, https://stopcor.org/zemelnoyi-reformy-boyatsya-ti-hto-proplachuye-mityngy/.

Prince, Todd. "As Washington Summit Nears, Disappointment Looms Over Ukraine-U.S. Relations," *Radio Free Europe/Radio Liberty,* August 29, 2021, https://www.rferl.org/a/biden-zelenskiy-ukraine-meeting/31433599.html.

Proskuryakov, Samuil. "The National Policy Institute has compiled a dossier accusing Sergei Korotkikh of working for Russian intelligence services. The dossier's author was later assaulted. Zaborona explains what it all means," *Zaborona,* January 21, 2021, https://zaborona.com/en/the-national-policy-institute-has-compiled-a-dossier-accusing-sergei-korotkikh-of-working-for-russian-intelligence-services-the-dossiers-author-was-later-assaulted/.

Ragozin, Leonid. "Brothers in Arms," *Coda Story,* June 29, 2017, https://www.codastory.com/disinformation/armed-conflict/brothers-in-arms/

Ravndal, Jacob Aasland. "From Bombs to Books, and Back Again? Mapping Strategies of Right-Wing Revolutionary Resistance," *Studies in Conflict & Terrorism,* 2021, DOI: 10.1080/1057610X.2021.1907897.

Rekawek, Kacper. "Career Break or New Career? Extremist Foreign Fighters in Ukraine," Counter Extremism Project (CEP), May 4, 2020, https://www.counterextremism.com/press/new-cep-report-career-break-or-new-career-extremist-foreign-fighters-ukraine.

Rekawek, Kacper. "Looks Can Be Deceiving: Extremism Meets Paramilitarism In Central And Eastern Europe," Counter Extremism Project (CEP), June 30, 2021, https://www.counterextremism.com/press/cep-report-examines-threats-extremism-paramilitarism-europe.

Removska, Olena. "Zelenskiy's 'De-Oligarchization' Goal Important, Path To Success 'Difficult,' U.S. Official Says," Radio Free Europe/Radio Liberty, July 24, 2021, https://www.rferl.org/a/zelenskiy-george-kent-ukraine/31375306.html

Reporter. "1 hrudnya u Zhytomyri "Azov" provede "Marsh Vidrodzhennia," November 25, 2015, https://reporter.zt.ua/2015/11/1-grudnya-u-Zhytomyri-Azov-provede-Marsh-Vidrodzhennya/.

Reporting Radicalism. "Dossiers," 2021, https://reportingradicalism.org/en/dossiers.

Risch, William Jay. "Heart of Europe, Heart of Darkness: Ukraine's Euromaidan and Its Enemies" In *The Unwanted Europeanness?: Understanding Division and Inclusion in Contemporary Europe,* edited by Branislav Radeljić, De Gruyter, 2021. https://doi.org/10.1515/9783110684216-006.

Roshchina, Viktoriya. "«Eto nastoyashchiy les v tsentre goroda»: udastsya li kiyevlyanam otstoyat' Protasov Yar," *Hromadske,* June 25, 2019, https://hromadske.ua/ru/posts/eto-nastoyashij-les-v-centre-goroda-udastsya-li-kievlyanam-otstoyat-protasov-yar.

Rossoliński-Liebe, Grzegorz. "The 'Ukrainian National Revolution' of 1941. Discourse and Practice of a Fascist Movement," *Kritika: Explorations in Russian and Eurasian History* vol. 12, no. 1, 2011.

Rossoliński-Liebe, Grzegorz. “The Fascist Kernel of Ukrainian Genocidal Nationalism.” *The Carl Beck Papers in Russian and East European Studies,* 0(2402)(2015), https://doi.org/10.5195/cbp.2015.204.

Rudling, Per Anders. "The OUN, the UPA and the Holocaust: A Study in the Manufacturing of Historical Myths." *The Carl Beck Papers in Russian and East European Studies* 2107 (2011).

Rudling, Per Anders. “Eugenics and Racial Anthropology in the Ukrainian Radical Nationalist Tradition.” *Science in Context* 32, no. 1 (2019): 67–91. doi:10.1017/S0269889719000048.

Scherban, Olena and Olena Halushka. “Ukraine’s Security Service reform plans under threat,” *Atlantic Council,* July 13, 2021, https://www.atlanticcouncil.org/blogs/ukrainealert/ukraines-security-service-reform-plans-under-threat/.

Schuster, Ruth. “‘Nomadic Warrior People of Scythia’ Is a Myth, Archaeologists Discover,” *Haaretz,* March 10, 2021, https://www.haaretz.com/archaeology/.premium.HIGHLIGHT-nomadic-warrior-people-of-scythia-is-a-myth-archaeologists-discover-1.9606726.

Sedgwick, Mark. “Introduction,” in *Key Thinkers of the Radical Right,* ed. Mark Sedgwick, Oxford University Press, 2019.

Seldin, Jeff. “White Supremacists Lead New Wave of Foreign Fighters,” *Voice of America,* September 30, 2019, https://www.voanews.com/a/usa_white-supremacists-lead-new-wave-foreign-fighters/6176687.html.

Sergatskova, Ekaterina. “The powerful and unpopular: Why the sudden resignation of Ukraine’s top police official is an important political event,” *Meduza,* July 15, 2021, https://meduza.io/en/feature/2021/07/15/the-powerful-and-unpopular.

Shak, Vladimir. "Ubiytsa berdyanskogo ATOshnika izbezhit tyur'my," *Mig*, September 3, 2019, https://mig.com.ua/ubijca-berdjanskogo-atoshnika-izbezhit-tjurmy/.

Shekhovtsov, Anton. "Wie Vetternwirtschaft ukrainischen Neonazis nützt," *Zeit Online*, December 11, 2014, https://www.zeit.de/politik/ausland/2014-12/ukraine-neonazis-vetternwirtschaft.

Shkandrij, Myroslav. "National democracy, the OUN, and Dontsovism: Three ideological currents in Ukrainian Nationalism of the 1930s–40s and their shared myth-system," *Communist and Post-Communist Studies* 1 September 2015; 48 (2-3): 209–216. doi: https://doi.org/10.1016/j.postcomstud.2015.06.002.

Skorkin, Konstantin, "Last Man Standing: How Avakov Survived in Ukraine," Carnegie Moscow Centre, February 12, 2020, https://carnegie.ru/commentary/81054.

Snyder, Timothy. "The Causes of Ukrainian-Polish Ethnic Cleansing 1943," *Past & Present*, 179, no. 1 (May 2003).

Spirin, Yevhen. "«Ne znimayte mene, mama pobachyt' – p*zdov vypyshe». U Kyyevi (mayzhe) nepomitno proyshla cherhova aktsiia «Azovs'koho rukhu»," *Babel'*, April 9, 2019, https://thebabel.com.ua/texts/28495-ne-znimayte-mene-mama-pobachit-p-zdov-vipishe-u-kiyevi-mayzhe-nepomitno-proyshla-chergova-akciya-azovskogo-ruhu.

Stone, Dan. *Goodbye To All That? The Story of Europe Since 1945*, Oxford University Press, 2014.

Stsiborskyi, Mykola. *Natsiokratiia*, 1935, http://ukrlife.org/-main/evshan/natiocracy.htm.

Subotić, Jelena. *Yellow Star, Red Star: Holocaust Remembrance after Communism*, Cornell University Press, 2019.

Sukhov, Oleg. "Foreigners Who Fight And Die For Ukraine: Russians join Ukrainians to battle Kremlin in Donbas," *Kyiv Post*, April 24, 2015, https://web.archive.org/web/20150427234735/http:/-www.kyivpost.com/content/ukraine/foreigners-who-fight-and-die-for-ukraine-russians-join-ukrainians-to-battle-kremlin-in-donbas-386999.html.

Sukhov, Oleg. "Corruption Accusations Dog Avakov, Ukraine's Top Cop," *Kyiv Post*, March 30, 2018, https://www.kyivpost.com/ukraine-politics/corruption-accusations-dog-avakov-ukraines-top-cop.html.

Sukhrakhov, Andrei. "Posle Marsha ravenstva v Khar'kove radikaly nachali otlavlivat' i izbivat' aktivistov. Politsiya grubykh narusheniy ne zafiksirovala," *Babel'*, September 15, 2019, https://thebabel.com.ua/ru/news/35730-marsh-ravenstva-v-harkove-radikaly-nachali-otlavlivat-aktivistov-posle-okonchaniya-shestviya.

Sumy National Agrarian University, "Proyshly «Shkolu muzhnosti»," September 20, 2019, http://gati.snau.edu.ua/news/924.

Synovitz, Ron. "V Ukrayini zakryvaiut' ochi na te, yak svit bachyt' ul'trapravyy rukh v krayini?" *Radio Svoboda*, December 31, 2020, https://www.radiosvoboda.org/a/ultrapravi-ukraina-svit-rosiya-propaganda/31028376.html.

Tarasiuk, Taras and Andreas Umland. "Unexpected Friendships: Cooperation of Ukrainian Ultra-Nationalists with Russian and Pro-Kremlin Actors," Institute for European, Russian, and Eurasian Studies (IERES), The George Washington University, September 8, 2021, https://www.illiberalism.org/unexpected-friendships-cooperation-of-ukrainian-ultra-nationalists-with-russian-and-pro-kremlin-actors/.

Thamm, Marianne. "Global alt-right exploiting SA's divisions and history," *Daily Maverick*, January 29, 2019, https://www.dailymaverick.co.za/article/2019-01-29-global-alt-right-exploiting-sas-divisions-and-history/.

TRAFO. "The Cossack Myth in Eastern Europe – Interview with Denys Shatalov," December 9, 2019, https://trafo.hypotheses.org/21007.

Tsybenko, Kateryna. ""Za shcho tebe povazhaty, yakshcho ty chornyy," Kameruntsya zasudyly na 5 rokiv za konflikt z ukrayintsem," *Gazeta.ua*, June 14, 2013, https://gazeta.ua/articles/np/_za-scho-tebe-povazhati-yakscho-ti-chornij-kameruncya-zasudili-na-5-rokiv-za-konflikt-z-ukrayincem/502352.

Tuck, Henry and Tanya Silverman. "The Counter-Narrative Handbook," Institute for Strategic Dialogue, 2016, https://www.isdglobal.org/wp-content/uploads/2016/06/-Counter-narrative-Handbook_1.pdf.

Tvernews, "V Tveri osuzhdena banda natsistov: lider poluchil pozhiznennyy srok," July 27, 2010, https://tvernews.ru-/news/80518/.

Ukrayinska Pravda, "SBU: Group of Bank Robbers Arrested, Including National Guard Serviceman," July 16, 2016, https://www.pravda.com.ua/eng/news/2016/07/16/7114947/.

Umland, Andreas. "Irregular Militias and Radical Nationalism in Post-Euromaydan Ukraine: The Prehistory and Emergence of the "Azov" Battalion in 2014," *Terrorism and Political Violence*, 31:1, 105-131, 2014, DOI: 10.1080/09546553.2018.1555974.

Verkkolehti Sarastus, "SARASTUS interview with Olena Semenyaka, international secretary of National Corps," April 2019, https://archive.fo/cRSIL.

Vernyhora, Anna. "Smert′ zasnovnyka «Azova»: nikhto ne viryt′ u samohubstvo," *Politeka,* October 18, 2017, https://politeka.net/-uk/news/521433-smert-osnovatelya-azova-nikto-ne-verit-v-samoubijstvo.

Vuiets, Pavlo, Mykhailo Hlukhovskyi and Stanislav Hruzdiev, "Andriy Bilets′kyy: Vlada zareydyla natsionalistychni hasla," *Glavcom,* November 29, 2018, https://glavcom.ua/country/politics/andriy-bileckiy-vlada-zareydila-nacionalistichni-gasla--548797.html

White, Mark. "Right-wing extremism is UK's fastest growing threat, says top counter-terror cop," *Sky News,* November 18, 2020, https://news.sky.com/story/right-wing-extremism-fastest-growing-threat-says-uks-top-cop-in-counter-terrorism-12135071.

Wilson, Andrew. "Modern Ukrainian nationalism: nationalist political parties in Ukraine 1988-1992," University of London, PhD dissertation, 1993, http://etheses.lse.ac.uk/1242/1/U056278.pdf.

Wilson, Andrew. *Ukrainian Nationalism in the 1990s: A Minority Faith,* Cambridge University Press, 1996

Yavir, Iryna. "Time to Party for Azov," *Political Critique,* November 7, 2016, http://politicalcritique.org/cee/ukraine/2016/time-to-party-for-azov/.

Yudina, Natalia. "The New Exile Strategy of Russian Nationalists," Institute for European, Russian, and Eurasian Studies (IERES), The George Washington University, December 18, 2020, https://www.illiberalism.org/the-new-exile-strategy-of-russian-nationalists/.

Zaitsev, Oleksandr. "Integral nationalism in the absence of a nation-state: The case of Ukraine," in *Conservatives and Right Radicals in Interwar Europe,* ed. Marco Bresciani, Routledge, 2020.

Zeltits, Raivis. "Interview with Olena Semenyaka, international secretary of National Corps (Ukraine)," *The New Nationalism*, July 15, 2019, https://archive.is/PgLrW.

Zik, "Natsionalizm - tse vidsutnist' ehoyizmu, - Bilets'kyy," November 22, 2017, https://zikua.tv/news/2017/11/22/natsionalizm__tse_vidsutnist_egoizmu__biletskyy_1210955.